MARY E ✔ KT-228-758

REFLECTING ON
ANNA KARENINA

ROUTLEDGE
London and New York

First published in 1989
by Routledge
11 New Fetter Lane, London EC4P 4EE

Simultaneously published in the USA and Canada
by Routledge
a division of Routledge, Chapman and Hall Inc.
29 West 35th Street, New York, NY 10001

Typeset in Baskerville 10/12 pt
by Witwell Limited, Southport
Printed in Great Britain
by Cox & Wyman Ltd, Reading

British Library Cataloguing in Publication Data

Evans, Mary, 1946-   .
Anna Karenina. – (Heroines?).
1. Fiction in Russian. Tolstoi, L.N. Anna Karenina –
Critical studies
I. Title   II. Series
891.73'3

Library of Congress Cataloging in Publication Data

Evans, Mary, 1946–
Anna Karenina/Mary Evans.
p.   cm.
1. Tolstoy, Leo, graf, 1828–1910. Anna Karenina.
2. Tolstoy, Leo, graf, 1828–1910 — Characters — Women.
3. Women in literature.
4. Sex role in literature.
5. Feminism in literature.
I. Title.
PG3365.A63E93 1989
891.73'3 — dc19
89–3588
CIP

ISBN 0-415-01719-X

CONTENTS

ACKNOWLEDGEMENTS

I am extremely grateful to those people who helped me, in one way or another, with the preparation of this book. Gill Davies provided the initial idea for the series and maintained a constant and supportive interest in its progress. Mrs Sue Macdonald typed the manuscript with care and interest; she was the ideal first reader. The many conversations I have had with Janet Sayers and Pat Macpherson have helped to clarify and illuminate some of the issues raised here. David Morgan read the manuscript with his usual sympathetic care. His interesting and critical observations made the project a happy one.

Chapter One

WHO IS ANNA? WHAT IS SHE?

ANNA KARENINA is one of the most famous women in fiction. Of all the heroines in western literature Anna represents, more than any other, the woman who gives all for love; in her case 'all' includes a social position and reputation, access to a beloved son, and finally her life. But the love that brings Anna to her death cannot be assumed to be a simple, straightforward matter of emotional preference. Anna's love for Vronsky is a complex mixture of heterosexual desire and need, which today – just as much as in nineteenth-century Russia – raises questions about all relationships between women and men, people of the same sex, and parents and their children. Anna, we must remember, loves not only Vronsky; she also loves, with great passion and conviction, her son Seriozha. Less passionately, but fondly, she also cares for her shiftless brother and his wife and had, at an earlier point in their marriage, been fond of her husband. Love is for Anna, as for most other people, a complex emotion which she experiences in many guises in relationship to more than one person.

Yet the love that comes to dominate her life, and to cause her death, is none of these lesser loves, but her passion for Vronsky. This passion ranks alongside those other great loves of fiction and myth – of Helen and Paris, of Antony and Cleopatra, and of Abelard and Héloïse. All these couples represent, in the same way as Anna and Vronsky, the high point of known and articulated heterosexual desire. All these couples are driven to desperate and socially disruptive actions by their love for one another and all, to a greater or lesser extent, bring disaster upon themselves and others. These great loves have little place in an orderly social world and yet they remain, paradoxically, our western measure of 'real', committed love. That all such loves defy rational action, justice to others and concern for the vulnerable counts for nothing against the powerful attraction of these mythical figures and their transcending passions.

The love of Anna and Vronsky (and Antony and Cleopatra *et al.*) is described by Tolstoy in what is generally regarded as one of the great novels of western literature. But if we view *Anna Karenina* in another light, other than that of accepted literary opinion, the essential narrative of the novel is simple, indeed vulgar, and we might well sympathize with Tolstoy's own view of the novel – that it was simple-minded, unworthy and a disgraceful distortion of human moral and emotional experiences. Given this permission by the author to view the novel as less than perfect it is possible to see how, in its essential elements, it resembles nothing less than a Mills and Boon romance – except, of course, that the ending is not that of a happily realized marriage. Otherwise, there is a great deal about the novel which is similar to the most banal romantic fiction: hero and heroine fall instantly in love (for no given reason) across a crowded room; hero follows heroine and declares his love in the middle of a snowstorm (thus allowing dramatic descriptions of the elements and natural forces); heroine nearly dies in childbirth; hero is inconsolable and the heroine's husband turns from an apparently reasonable, if unattractive, man into an embodiment of all that is repressive and narrow-minded in western bourgeois society. Just as there is apparently no place in the social world for the love of Catherine and Heathcliff in *Wuthering Heights* (and again snowstorms and high winds are used as metaphors for passion and desire), so there is eventually no place for Anna and Vronsky. Despite Vronsky's best efforts to become a bourgeois *gentilhomme* and live the life of a country squire he cannot avoid the temptations of the corrupted social world of aristocratic society any more than Anna can emancipate herself from its values and judgements.

So what we have in *Anna Karenina* is a tale that in some

respects does resemble the simplest romantic fiction – a tale of a great love between a man and a woman, a love that conforms to those various clichés about love moving mountains and even, on occasions, the earth. Unlike romantic fiction, however, Tolstoy's novel contains an extraordinarily rich and vivid portrayal of part of a vanished society, and endless material for re-interpretation and speculation. *Anna Karenina* can be read as a novel about Tsarist Russia, a novel about social convention and its crushing effect on emotional life, a moral tale about the danger of loving outside socially accepted and agreed boundaries, or as a discussion not merely about love, but also about life, and how to live it. All these readings and many others are possible.

But what concerns us here is less the novel itself than the figure of Anna, a woman who can be variously interpreted as a demonstration of women's capacity for passion and sexual desire on the one hand and on the other, as a woman who is so trapped by conventional – and ultimately conservative – notions about romantic love that she abandons all other possible avenues of action. Thus, we can see Anna as either a deeply liberating, and liberated, figure, or as an equally deeply imprisoned and repressed figure. For the first point of view we can argue that Anna defies the mundane and material world for a vision of the ideal; for the second point of view we can argue that Anna traps herself in a personal prison, a prison in which her love, and her lover, are the gaolers. To these two, extreme, interpretations we can add interpretations derived from particular ideological persuasions: for example, to a socialist Anna might be seen as the personification of all that is futile and socially dangerous about bourgeois love and romance. It is difficult to imagine that Anna's plight would receive much sympathy in the context of contemporary China. Here is a woman who, after all, is about nothing less than a highly individualized love which places all other considerations – social and personal responsibilities in particular – in second place. To feminists, Anna can be seen as less a heroine than a victim, a victim of all that is most debilitating, corrupting and repressive about heterosexual love. Anna, many feminists would remark, ends the novel dead: the inequalities between women and men that constitute a major feature of western society are vividly portrayed in the novel – bourgeois heterosexuality kills women, and ruins men.

Any reading of *Anna Karenina*, and any interpretation of Anna herself, will reveal as much about the reader as about the novel and the character. For example, in his essay, on *Anna Karenina*, F. R. Leavis cites one particularly vivid example of the self-revelation that can occur. D. H. Lawrence, Leavis tells us, apparently happily (and unselfconsciously) remarked that 'No-one in the world is anything but delighted when Vronsky gets Anna Karenina'. Leavis dissents from this view, and goes on to chastise Lawrence for what he describes as Lawrence's failure to understand the complexities of the novel. Lawrence receives further admonishment for his remark that: 'Why, when you look at it, all the tragedy comes from Vronsky's and Anna's fear of society ... they couldn't live in the pride of their sincere passion, and spit in Mother Grundy's eye. And that, that cowardice, was the real "sin". The novel makes it obvious, and knocks all old Leo's teeth out.' As Lawrence is an author whom Leavis admires, he does not condemn this remark outright; he suggests, however, that perhaps Lawrence was a trifle heavy-handed in his judgement of Tolstoy.[1] But Leavis on Lawrence, and Lawrence on *Anna Karenina*, reveal as much about the preoccupations of the critics themselves as about the novel: part of Lawrence's project in his literary work was to defend the primacy of passion and passionate sexuality against social conventions; equally, Leavis's preoccupation was to demonstrate a moral continuity in the realist novels of nineteenth- and twentieth-century Europe. This essay is written without – at least knowingly – the same kind of crusading spirit that inspired Lawrence and Leavis, but it is written from the belief that the ideology of western romantic love is worth, at the very least, critical evaluation. Indeed, if ever an indictment of romantic love was necessary, Tolstoy provides it; romance kills, is literally what the narrative of *Anna Karenina* tells us.

It is doubtful if the author himself would have described the cause of Anna's death as romance: indeed, he might well have accused literary and social critics of mealy-mouthed fastidious-ness in naming the passion of Vronsky and Anna as romance. Sexual passion might well be a better description that would accord more closely to Tolstoy's own understanding of his central characters, and of similar relationships between men and women in real life. The novel is, however, sufficiently coloured by Tolstoy's own experience to suggest that he did not see the relationship between Anna and Vronsky in any single sense. Certainly physical, sexual passion played a part, but so did other needs and desires – for social confirmation, for emotional intimacy, for intellectual and social companionship and even for the experience of integrity – an experience that was critically denied by the formal, and elaborate, social world in which Anna and Vronsky lived. We know from biographical and autobiographical material that Tolstoy experienced certain diffi-culties in his relationships with women (not to mention, of course, the difficulties that women experienced in their dealings with Tolstoy). His own marriage, to a woman twelve years younger than himself, resembled in many ways the relationship between Levin and Kitty in *Anna Karenina*, in that Tolstoy invested in his wife (as did Levin in Kitty) his hopes for reliving his relationship with his mother. The dead, venerated mother was for Tolstoy, as much as for Levin, the embodiment of all that was saintly in women. Society women for Tolstoy, as for Levin, were persons of fascination and terror: it was only with young women – indeed adolescent girls – that author and character could enter into marriage. Tolstoy does not tell us whether or not Levin saw each instance of marital sexual intercourse in the same way that Tolstoy did, as a fall from grace so horrible as to be deplored and the occasion for recrimination and self-loathing. But he does suggest that Levin experiences guilt at the results, for Kitty, of sexuality – namely the pain of childbirth and the debilitating preoccupation of childcare. Indeed, throughout *Anna Karenina* male guilt is a central theme. Vronsky and Levin both endure anguish and anger as Anna and Kitty bear their children, and Levin is endlessly, and generously, guilty about the way that other men (for example Oblonsky and Levin's brother) behave towards the women with whom they are involved.

But what makes men behave badly towards women is what Tolstoy saw, in both his own life and in fiction, as the curse of physical desire. Vronsky cannot but desire Anna, Oblonsky cannot resist, amongst others, his children's governess, and Levin himself – the eventual paterfamilias and benign landlord – spent a youth as apparently dissolute as that of any aristocratic young man. Vronsky and Oblonsky do not, eventually, lie crushed beneath the wheels of a train, but our last sight of Vronsky is of a man broken in spirit and condemned to a life of self-loathing, whilst Oblonsky's final fate is to become a more pathetic version of the good living fellow who greeted us at the beginning of the novel. What saves Oblonsky and Levin (and Tolstoy himself) is a household and a family. Thus we enter a perceptual world in which romance and sex are portrayed in fiction not as the glue of social life and social relationships but as the acid that rots and destroys the very fabric of social order and cohesion.

This pattern of perceiving sexuality as disruptive is a common theme in western fiction. From the days of *Clarissa* to the feminist novel of the late 1980s there are endless examples of novels organized around the theme of the disruption of the bourgeois order by sexuality. And amongst the novels that deal with this theme are some of the west's greatest contributions to fiction: *Wuthering Heights, Doctor Faustus, Madame Bovary, Mansfield Park, The Mill on the Floss* are a few examples of novels which are organized around the failure (or impossibility) of characters to resist the temptations of physical desire. The objects of desire may be unattractive in worldy or conventional terms, but in terms of the passions they arouse their power amounts almost to magic – a magic that many major novelists cannot themselves define. Two examples illustrate the realization by novelists that the power to seduce has little to do with ordinary standards of beauty. The first is Tolstoy's own tacit acknowledgement in *Anna Karenina* that it is extremely difficult to name in precise terms Anna's fatal allure. John Bayley tells us, in his essay on *Anna Karenina* in *Tolstoy and the Novel*, that in the first draft of the novel Tolstoy described Anna thus:

She had a low forehead, a short, almost retroussé nose, and was far too plump – a little more and she would have seemed monstrous. Indeed, without the great black eyelashes which made her grey eyes wonderful, the black curls on her forehead, a vigorous grace of movement like her brother's, and small feet and hands, she would have been downright ugly.[2]

In the final version of the novel Tolstoy has abandoned the attempt to describe Anna's features in any detail and tells the reader, instead, about the impression that Anna conveys:

Vronsky followed the guard to the carriage, and at the door of the compartment had to stop and make way for a lady. . . . He begged her pardon and was about to enter the carriage but felt he must have another look at her – not because of her beauty, nor on account of the elegance and unassuming grace of her whole figure, but because of something tender and caressing in her lively face as she passed him. As he looked round, she too turned her head. Her brilliant grey eyes, shadowed by thick lashes, gave him a friendly, attentive look, as though she were recognising him, and then turned to the approaching crowd as if in search of someone. In that brief glance Vronsky had time to notice the suppressed animation which played over her face and flitted between her sparkling eyes and the slight smile curving her red lips. It was as though her nature was so brimming over with something that against her will it expessed itself now in a radiant look, now in a smile. She deliberately shrouded the light in her eyes but in spite of herself it gleamed in the faintly perceptible smile.[3]

The crucial sentence here is 'it was as though her nature was so brimming over with something that against her will it expressed itself now in a radiant look, now in a smile.' Because it is in this sentence that Tolstoy suggests, as Jane Austen, George Eliot, Emily Brontë and Thomas Mann were also to do, that what makes individuals attractive is the vitality that they possess, and that apparent easy access to the direct expression of emotion and feeling that is generally either absent or buried in more mundane individuals. It is, in a sense, a certain childishness about the Anna Kareninas of literature that makes them appealing: just as children express their emotions with a directness that confounds and disturbs the adult world, so Anna, and even more her brother Oblonsky, are creatures with an unbroken sense of the consolations of the sensual world and the importance of maintaining their access to them – in Anna's case through her relationship with Vronsky, in Oblonsky's case through making sure that all trials in life are mediated by excellent dinners. Indeed, in the early pages of the novel we meet Anna and Oblonsky as creatures of comfort; in the midst of domestic drama Oblonsky still enjoys the consolation of clean clothes and mourns, as much as his wife's unhappiness, the disruption of his domestic order, whilst Anna, returning home to a husband of whom she is at best only tolerant, consoles herself with the comforts of a new novel and her well ordered and well chosen possessions.

So Anna, we might conclude, has a strong sense of the physical and the material world, and an ability to communicate to others the possibilities of sensual pleasure of all kinds. Similarly, in describing Henry Crawford, the heart-breaker of *Mansfield Park*, Jane Austen tells us that he was, at first glance, rather plain, but on subsequent meetings, and particulary in his conversation, could convey a strong sense of energy and sensitivity – precisely what Tolstoy notes of Anna. Thus Anna descends from the train after her first meeting with Vronsky, with a 'light, sure step' and embraces her brother with a gesture that 'struck Vronsky with its decision and grace'. Equally, Henry Crawford is so articulate and at ease with the written and spoken word that it is a pleasure for people to listen to him talk, or read. Both characters, Henry Crawford and Anna Karenina, are portrayed by their respective authors as people wholly in command of their performance in action and words. That this is not the case forms the plot of both *Anna Karenina* and *Mansfield Park* – both characters cannot, in fact, contain their energy or organize its expression in ways that are socially and morally acceptable.

But the parallels between *Mansfield Park* and *Anna Karenina* do not stop at the personalities of Henry and Anna. Two further points are strikingly similar between these otherwise disparate novels: Henry Crawford, like Anna, has a sibling who throws into relief many of his characteristics and indeed suggests his failings, and both Henry and his sister, and Anna and her brother come from unstable, if privileged, families. The expressed opinions of Mary Crawford predict the moral failings which Henry will eventually reveal, whilst Oblonsky's excursions from the straight and narrow road of domestic life suggest Anna's much more fatal, and decisive, departure from wifely virtue. Vice, it would seem, runs in families, and particularly families that have no established or settled home. 'Vronsky', Tolstoy writes with some of the vigour of a twentieth-century child-care officer, 'had never had a real home-life.'[4] What is more, Tolstoy goes on, 'In his youth his mother had been a brilliant society woman and during her husband's life-time, and still more after his death, had had many love affairs, which everyone knew about.'[5] Vronsky, Anna, and Oblonsky, and Mary and Henry Crawford, all live apparently settled lives, and indeed by the relative standards of their contemporary societies, particularly privileged lives, but they are unable to make those personal and emotional decisions which secure the continuity and the harmony of social life and the stability of social relationships. Vronsky, Henry Crawford, and Oblonsky are adulterers – as indeed is Anna herself – whilst Mary Crawford although technically free from sin is as morally culpable as her brother.

So one of the first features about Anna is her rootlessness. Tolstoy tells us almost nothing about Anna's childhood and adolescence. All we know is that she was married off to Karenin and spent her married life in the highest social circles of St Petersburg. Anna, unlike Kitty and Dolly, has no ties to a country estate, no large family and very little domestic and personal baggage of the kind that accompanies the two sisters. In Tolstoy, as in Austen, we find an association of city life with vice and country life with simplicity and true virtue. It is perfectly possible for worthy characters to move between the two worlds, but it is impossible for a worthy character to have no understanding of the moral importance of the countryside. Both authors are writing, of course, of pre-industrial societies, and the countryside, for Austen and Tolstoy's contemporaries, was the major source of sustenance and wealth. But apart from this fact of pre-industrial life both authors are arguing for a moral perception of the value of rural society – not because turning the sod is in itself a moral activity (although passages in *Anna Karenina* come close to this position) but because the failure to care for the land – the wealth of the world, and the means of provision for individuals – is to turn one's back on those mutual associations and responsibilities which bind societies and families together. Anna and Vronsky, Tolstoy tells us, cannot settle to country life (nor indeed can Oblonsky) and maternity fails to provide for Anna a way of life. She is passionately fond of her son, but largely disinterested in her daughter by Vronsky.

What we know about Anna is that she is a creature of the social, urban world – a woman whose first passion is for her son, and whose interests are centred around her son and her own person. Anna is not, in anything like the same sense as Dolly or Kitty, a housekeeper: it is difficult to imagine her making jam on a hot summer's afternoon or tying up her hair in an untidy knot to take her children swimming. Anna appears, at every scene and on every occasion, beautifully dressed and arranged. Only towards the end of the novel does her narcissism begin to diminish, and then there is only the merest hint that pride and interest in her appearance – and the impression that she will make – is beginning to falter. Even then, it is not so much Anna's interest in her appearance that begins to decline, but her ability to maintain the poise and the grace that had been so essential a part of her charm and seductiveness. As Anna becomes more aggressive, more brittle, much less polite and more demanding in her relations with Vronsky, so we see the vitality that was once so attractive turned into a defeating, although no less agile, energy. The woman who had once been able to subdue and to claim Vronsky's feelings becomes the person who now can do nothing to please him. The transformation is neither final, nor complete. Only a few hours before her suicide Anna still appears as lovely as ever to Kitty, but to Vronsky she has become a source of irritation, a person who is capable of vulgarity and the kind of behaviour that has no place in fantasies of the perfect woman.

The implication of that last sentence is, in fact, that Anna is a fantasy, a fantasy of both Tolstoy and Vronsky. Anna's rootlessness, her distance from, and lack of interest in, domestic and maternal concerns place her not amongst women in general but apart from them. It is not that women are naturally interested in domestic life and the care of children, but such has been the sexual division of labour that in all western societies women have been placed – like it or not – in the household. Tolstoy's fantasies about a woman who can inspire male desire (and even Levin is forced to admit to Anna's seductive powers) have no place for the realities of female experience which commonly include not merely the love for children (an emotion which Anna was certainly capable of) but the care of them. Dolly and Kitty consult each other about the care of Kitty's baby. Ironically, it is only because of Karenin's intervention that Anna and Vronsky's daughter survives. Dolly and Kitty are preoccupied with the details of their households; Anna has little to do with any domestic tasks other than those that include her wardrobe. Indeed, for any task that is related to her narcissism Anna has considerable energy – an interest in her clothes is but one aspect of the cultivation of self which surrounds her. It is predictable, certainly in psychoanalytical terms, that this woman should love so dearly her son (albeit by a despised husband) and be so disinterested in a daughter (albeit by an adored lover). It is, moreover, a feeling that Tolstoy emphasizes by his portrayal of the physical characteristics of Anna's children. Seriozha is a complete, finished child – recognizably a young man, whilst the baby daughter is a plump bundle of polymorphous perversity. The son can give the mother 'almost physical pleasure' with his caresses, whilst the daughter can offer nothing, and can only demand.

And the demands of her daughter do not, for Anna, constitute moral imperatives in the same way as do the demands of their children for Dolly and Kitty. So this most apparently feminine woman, and certainly a woman who can appeal strongly to men, is not in the general, conventional sense a maternal woman. A passionate mother of a son perhaps, but a woman who specifically and categorically refuses her lover more children and whose relations with her own are at best fleeting.

From the point of view of Seriozha and Ani, Anna is anything but an ideal mother; Tolstoy tells us that Seriozha has to develop a protective dislike of his mother in order to come to terms with her loss, and the eventual fate of Ani is one of those fictional loose-ends which Tolstoy fails, forgets or cannot bring himself to conclude.

The relationship of Anna to her living children, and to those prospective children which she might have with Vronsky, portrays an assumptive world that exactly matches the arrangements of the bourgeois family in both the nineteenth and the twentieth century. Anna – a creature who embodies western male fantasies about the ultimately seductive woman – is not a woman preoccupied with the care of children. Dolly and Kitty, on the other hand, are the absolutely and utterly committed mothers of bourgeois families. They do not, however, inspire in their husbands or bring into existence those heights (or depths) of heterosexual passion that exist between Anna and Vronsky. Maternal love, and the ability to inspire and share sexual passion, are thus neatly compartmentalized and no one realizes this more forcefully than Anna – and indeed Dolly. When Dolly goes to visit Anna at Vronsky's country estate she has a conversation with her in which Anna reveals that she is deliberately and consciously practising birth control. Dolly is amazed by the revelation:

> 'Impossible!' exclaimed Dolly, opening her eyes wide.
> For her this was one of those discoveries the consequences and inferences of which are too vast to take in at a moment's notice. She would have to reflect a great, great deal upon it.
> This discovery, suddenly throwing light on all those families of one or two children, which had hitherto been so in-comprehensible to her, aroused so many ideas, reflections and contradictory emotions that she was unable to say anything, and could only stare at Anna wide-eyed with amazement. This was precisely what she had been dreaming of on the way to Anna's that morning, but now that she learned that it was a possibility she was horrified. It seemed to her too simple a solution for too complicated a problem.[6]

Anna's justification for her actions – a justification that is apparently as necessary for Tolstoy as it is for Dolly – is that it is only through sexual attraction that she can maintain Vronsky's fidelity and loyalty. As she says 'he loves me as long as he loves me.'

But if Dolly is at first amazed, and slightly shocked, by Anna's revelation she is also both intrigued by this device for maintaining male sexual fidelity and yet, ultimately, not convinced of its effectiveness. Assessing the relationship between Vronsky and Anna, in the light of this intimate knowledge, Dolly muses to herself that if sexual attraction is the fundamental premise of Vronsky and Anna's relationship, then it is a relationship that is doomed to end. Thus Dolly reasons to herself that

> If that is all he looks for, he will find dresses and manners still more attractive and charming. And however white and shapely her bare arms, however beautiful her stately figure and her eager face under that black hair, he will find others still lovelier, just as my poor dear reprobate of a husband does.[7]

So what we are presented with in this conversation is a perception of the organization of relations between men and women that supposes that the way in which those relationships are maintained is not through love, passion, and romance or whatever other name is used to describe highly individualized heterosexual attraction, but through general, shared commitments to a household and children. Dolly, who has endured seven pregnancies, the loss of two children and the certain knowledge of her husband's infidelity, nevertheless leaves Anna and Vronsky's household with the conviction that she is in a far stronger social, and emotional, position than Anna. Her husband's debts, her concerns about her children and her own sometimes failing energies are as nothing compared to the fact that Anna, in order to maintain her world, and her happiness, has to continue to attract Vronsky.

It is, of course, true that Anna's situation, unlike that of Kitty and Dolly, is insecure because of the illicit nature of her relationship with Vronsky. Living as she does, as Vronsky's mistress, Anna is excluded from society and hence even more dependent on Vronsky's approval and company. The couple are forced to live, after Anna leaves Karenin, as exiles – at first literally exiles from Russia and subsequently as exiles and social outcasts within their own society. But it is Anna, rather than Vronsky, who carries the weight of social disapproval. It is Anna, not Vronsky, who is publicly humiliated and has to spend her days in hotel rooms and rural seclusion. Yet such social disapproval as Anna meets is hardly specifically Russian or aristocratic: Mrs Gaskell, for example, refused to meet George Eliot because of Eliot's relationship with George Lewes and, in this century, it is only in the last twenty years that divorce has ceased to carry an intense social stigma. In Anna's case a divorce from Karenin could have been arranged, and there are extensive discussions in the novel where various characters air their views on the matter and propose solutions. In all these discussions, however, it is Anna who apparently vacillates most – and this vacillation heightens the impression that Tolstoy is creating in Anna an idealization rather than a real person – in this case, someone who represents all that is seductive, irresistible and potentially destructive about female sexuality. If Anna was properly 'organized' into Vronsky's wife she would become an ordinary person, a woman with a husband, a household and children. As Vronsky's mistress Anna remains a symbol of all those possibilities about sexuality which are most threatening to social order. Indeed, if Anna were to become Vronsky's wife, with proper arrangements for a divorce and the care of Seriozha and Ani, then what began as a grand passion would be translated into yet another bourgeois household – a household and a marriage which would, in its own turn, run all the same risks as that of the Levins and the Oblonskys.

So Anna and Vronsky remain unmarried, and Tolstoy maintains, to the very end of the novel, the passionate nature of the affair between them. But, by the end, the passion has turned sour and bitter; Anna has become suspicious and distrustful of Vronsky and Vronsky in his turn has become resentful and bored by the constraints that Anna imposes upon him. With no profession, and no place in the world, Vronsky becomes dissatisfied and lonely; used to the male camaraderie of the barracks and the officers' club he finds it hard to spend his days in the company only of Anna and a few individuals. Removed from the world which sustained his capacity for romantic associations with women, Vronsky rapidly becomes un-interested in romance. Here, then, is another of those paradoxes which Tolstoy points to: that the social conditions and circumstances which are most likely to create the need for emotional intimacy are precisely those conditions and circumstances which are also the graveyard of such hopes and desires. Anna's need for intimacy, for physical affection, and for emotional experience are all created, to a significant extent, by her position as a wife in a bourgeois marriage, a situation in which it is expected that women will act primarily as wives and mothers and turn away from other inclinations to act as sexual beings. Vronsky's perception of women, as a bachelor who spends most of his time with other men, is essentially romantic and idealistic. He does not associate with somen who make demands of him or who ask that he should act as a dutiful and faithful husband with household and social obligations. His love for Anna is intense and all-consuming, but it is, in a social sense, unplaced and at odds with social expectations.

The social conventions of bourgeois and aristocratic society placed sexual desire and attraction apart from the ordinary, everyday life of the household *Anna Karenina* was first published, in instalments, between 1875 and 1877, just a few years before Engels, in *The Origin of the Family, Private Property and the State*, wrote a non-fictional analysis of the compartmentalization of desire, love, and the establishment and organization of the bourgeois household which in many ways resembles that of Tolstoy. Engels is concerned, of course, to trace relationships between the ownership of private property and the organization of the bourgeois family and the state in ways which Tolstoy is not, but nevertheless a passage in Engels' work echoes Tolstoy's own discussion of bourgeois marriage. Writing of the introduction of monogamy and the bourgeois family Engels states:

Two permanent social figures, previously unknown, appear on

the scene along with monogamy – the wife's paramour and the cuckold. The men had gained the victory over the women, but the act of crowning the victor was magnanimously undertaken by the vanquished. Adultery – proscribed, severely penalised, but irrepressible – became an unavoidable social institution alongside of monogamy and hetaerism. The assured paternity of children was now, as before, based, at best, on moral conviction; and in order to solve the insoluble contradiction, Article 312 of the Code Napoléon decreed, 'L'enfant concu pendant le mariage a pour père le mari,' 'a child conceived during marriage has for its father the husband.' This is the final outcome of three thousand years of monogamy.[8]

Adultery, as Tolstoy describes it, and Engels defines it, is in Engels' words 'irrepressible' – an unavoidable consequence of marriages organized primarily around property and the maintenance of social order.

In their different ways, therefore, both Engels and Tolstoy recognize that the deceits, failings, and miseries of many bourgeois marriages are less the fault of individuals than of the particular ways in which societies organize sexuality. Tolstoy's account of the lives of Anna and Vronsky, Kitty and Levin, and the Oblonskys throws into vivid relief the whole continuum of the bourgeois experience of marriage: Kitty and Levin represent the realized ideal of a conventionally happy and conventionally realized marriage, the Oblonskys represent the maintained, if flawed and at times unhappy, bourgeois marriage, and Anna and Vronsky stand for both the hope of the absolutely happy relationship between men and women and the impossibility, within the existing social order, of realizing that hope. The happiness of Anna and Vronsky is based on the hope of transcendence and unity, the happiness of Kitty and Levin on separate spheres of daily life. Whilst we may long for those relationships which seem to promise transcendence and unity it is part of Tolstoy's concern to suggest to his readers that it is only through separation, and the recognition of separation, that individuals can achieve happiness. On the final page of *Anna Karenina* Levin makes his decisive choice for the future of his relationship with Kitty. While gazing and musing at the stars, Levin's reverie is interrupted by Kitty. About to tell her his thoughts, Levin stops, and says to himself: '"No, I had better not speak of it," he thought, as she passed in before him. "It is a secret for me alone, of vital importance for me, and not to be put into words."'[9]

So Levin, unlike Anna, opts not to share all his emotional life with the person closest to him. Since Levin and Anna are the two most complex people in the novel, and the people who struggle and agonize most over their fate and their actions, it is reasonable to suggest that each represents, for Tolstoy, different possibilities of human happiness and misery. Anna, like Levin, is searching for a meaning for her life: she, like Levin, first appears in the novel in a state of discontent. Her realization and recognition of her discontent is first articulated when she returns home from Oblonsky's and sees Karenin awaiting her at the station. In a moment of sudden clarity she looks at Karenin and her feelings crystalize:

> A disagreeable sensation oppressed her heart when she met his fixed and weary gaze, as though she had expected to find him different. She was particularly impressed by the feeling of dissatisfaction with herself which she experienced when they met. It was that old familiar feeling, like a consciousness of hypocrisy, which she experienced in her relations with her husband. But hitherto she had not taken note of the feeling, whereas now she was clearly and painfully aware of it.[10]

And later that evening, her feelings take a more material form:

> 'After all, he's a good man; upright, kind, and remarkable in his own line', Anna said to herself when she had returned to her room, as though defending him from attack – from the accusation that he was not lovable. 'But why is it his ears stick out so oddly? Or has he had his hair cut too short?'[11]

The visits to Moscow of Anna and Levin – with which *Anna Karenina* begins – are both revealing, crucial, and predictive. Anna's visit to the Oblonskys brings a certain uneasy peace to their household, but far more significant, the visit is the occasion of her first meeting with Vronsky, a meeting that arouses in her feelings which she can neither fully name nor

control. Thus Anna returns home dissatisfied and uneasy, her
life disturbed and her relations with her husband fatally upset
by the comparison of Karenin and Vronsky. Levin, on the other
hand, returns home in a state of equal irritable dissatisfaction,
but as soon as he arrives at his estate, his dissatisfactions –
unlike Anna's – disappear:

> The next morning Levin left Moscow and towards evening
> arrived home. On the way back in the train he chatted politics
> and the new railways with his fellow-passengers, and felt
> depressed, just as he had in Moscow, by the confusion in his
> mind, dissatisfaction with himself, and a vague sense of shame.
> But when he got out at his station and saw his one-eyed
> coachman, Ignat, with the collar of his coat turned up; when he
> caught sight in the dim light from the station windows of his
> own upholstered sledge, his horses with their plaited tails, and
> the harness with its rings and tassels; and when Ignat, while they
> were getting ready to start, began telling him the village news –
> how the contractor had arrived and Para had called – Levin felt
> that little by little his confusion was clearing up and his shame
> and self-dissatisfaction were melting away.[12]

These two homecomings reveal recurrent sources of irritation
and satisfaction in the lives of Tolstoy's central characters. Levin,
who has achieved none of his objects in Moscow (most centrally
securing the agreement of Kitty to a marriage), is nevertheless
reassured by the sight of his home, his property, and his place
in the world. All these things confirm his sense of worth, his
identity, and his optimism. For Anna, on the other hand, her
home, her child, and her husband are disappointing. Far from
being the balm for her disturbed spirits that she had hoped for
all these places and people are less reassuring and less
acceptable than she had expected. Even the adored Seriozha is,
in the flesh, less than perfect. Anna, the woman who represents
to Tolstoy all that is fascinating and seductive about women, is
thus presented, in the earliest pages of the novel, as a deeply
discontented woman.

But equally early in the novel Tolstoy has proposed to us a
reason, or set of reasons, for the profound dissatisfactions of his
central character. Anna, as we have seen, is emotionally isolated

in a way that Dolly and Kitty are not. Both the Shcherbatsky sisters are protected by their relationship with each other and their family. Oblonsky is allowed the extramarital relationships and personal indulgences by a culture that sanctions male infidelity and hedonism. But infidelity and hedonism in women are different matters. Wordly women were certainly known in pre-revolutionary Russia, and Vronsky's mother did not become a social outcast by her affairs. But she did not – as Anna did – make these affairs a public matter or compromise the accepted norms of the bourgeois world by parading an illicit love and destroying a marriage. So what we have is a woman who desires – and who to a great extent stands for desire – living in a culture that denies female romance except on those terms that are domestically acceptable – terms which, to Anna, actually deny the possibility of the realization of her desires. Anna's dilemma, the social and emotional place of female sexual desire in bourgeois society, is a dilemma that Tolstoy states explicitly. Equally explicitly, he proposes the dangers to the social world of such desire, and the danger both of attempting to realize and fulfil sexual desire and of abandoning those social relationships and social interests which might provide alternative, although far from identical, interest.

When Anna and Vronsky finally become lovers, Anna turns to Vronsky and says, 'Everything is over ... I have nothing but you left. Remember that.' The remark is perhaps one of the two essential clues that Tolstoy provides to Anna's eventual fate: her perception of her situation as that of final, unchanging commitment and of complete abandonment of everything else that had ever existed in her life. The phrase 'Remember that' is the directive to Vronsky that he cannot fulfil, and of which she is so aggressively to remind him. Vronsky's fate, as well as Anna's, is sealed in this exchange. It is only later in the novel that Tolstoy gives us the second clue to Anna's eventual fate when he tells us that Vronsky 'began to feel that the realization of his desires brought him no more than a grain of sand out of the mountain of bliss he had expected. It showed him the eternal error men make in imagining that happiness consists in the realization of their desires.' We are told then, that for Anna becoming Vronsky's mistress is so irrevocable, so decisive, that it changes all else, whereas for Vronsky the satisfaction of being Anna's lover, although most deeply desired, is not deeply satisfying.

The question then arises of why this should be the case. Here are two people (four if we include the disappointments that Kitty and Levin also find in their marriage) who have no material problems, who have a deep concern for each other and every apparent ability to act rationally. Yet one of them commits suicide, the other we leave setting off on a potentially dangerous military mission. Some of the reasons for Anna and Vronsky's eventual misery are structural – their failure to marry and achieve social respectability and re-integration and the problem of Anna's relationship with her son. But Tolstoy suggests to us that easier divorce would not make this pair happy; something more is at stake than the problems of an antiquated set of marriage laws. What might be at stake is in part contained in that bleak sentence in which Vronsky acknowledges that achieving his desires has not made him happy. Some forty years later Freud was to write that 'We must reckon with the possibility that something in the nature of the sexual instinct itself is unfavourable to the realisation of complete satisfaction'.[13] This quotation is taken from an essay whose title ('On the Universal Tendency to Debasement in the Sphere of Love') might be an appropriate sub-title for *Anna Karenina*, a novel that demonstrates, above all else, the fallacies of romance.

So both Tolstoy and Freud share the view that sexual attraction, and sexual experience, are as inherently disappointing as they are dangerous and disturbing. Writing of Freud's views on romantic love, Elizabeth Wilson provides a discussion that is directly relevant to *Anna Karenina* and its themes when she remarks that:

> Freud was a great debunker of romantic love: 'Sexual over-estimation is the origin of the peculiar state of being in love, a state suggestive of a neurotic compulsion' (Freud, 1948).

On the other hand, Freud saw desire as incapable of being fulfilled and indeed as compelling precisely because of the obstacles in its way. 'An obstacle is required in order to heighten libido; and where natural resistances to satisfaction have not been sufficient men have at all times erected conventional ones so as to be able to enjoy love' (Freud, 1977). Since Freud perceived erotic love as rooted in the infant's love of its parental figures, which in turn grows, according to him, out of satisfaction of the baby's bodily needs (ultimately the need for survival), he viewed the state of being in love as a development from narcissism. The individual in love abandons narcissism, but seeks indirect satisfaction for it by projecting it onto the idealised love object, thereby in a sense reappropriating the love of self.[14]

Anna and Vronsky, from the information about them that Tolstoy provides, meet all the conditions for the compulsive neurotics doomed to disappointment that Freud describes. Anna is a woman whose marriage is deeply unsatisfying, but who is presented to us as a woman capable of passionate involvement, not least with herself and with the self-conscious presentation of herself. Karenin proves that necessary obstacle whom Freud describes as so essential to eroticism. Anna's refusal of a divorce we can therefore read as her unconscious realization that without Karenin much of the erotic tension and understanding between herself and Vronsky would disappear. But this refusal is also, and paradoxically, a refusal of Vronsky that in turn alienates Vronsky from her. Karenin is less necessary for Vronsky than for Anna; what Anna does in refusing the possibility of a divorce is in a sense to refuse to recognize the legitimacy and autonomy of Vronsky himself. Such is Anna's narcissism that she cannot allow the possibility of a relationship with Vronsky that depends on anything other than his passion for her. Vronsky's wish that their relationship, their child, and their future children, be legitimated would, in Anna's eyes, be a translation of a relationship that is personally and emotionally satisfying into a relationship that is socially convenient.

But, of course, and here we come to that issue which must make Anna an ultimately sympathetic figure for feminists (or anyone committed to sexual equality), Anna can become a legitimate person in an ordered relationship, only on patriarchal terms and in a patriarchal society. If she consents to a divorce, she is granted a divorce by male charity and to secure male interests, namely Vronsky's interests that Ani, and the children (particularly the son) that he and Anna might have become legitimate. Legitimate children then bear his name (Ani, although Vronsky's child, bears Karenin's name) and can inherit his property. The relationship between Vronsky and Anna would thus be translated from a relationship founded, at least initially, on mutual commitment and affection, to a relationship based on the laws of class society. The eventual tragedy of the novel is that Anna, the figure who stands for female sexuality and vitality, can only fulfil those attributes within the context of structures ordered by male, and bourgeois, interests. Vronsky, as much as Karenin, fails Anna in that he as much as the loathed and feared husband has no real perception of a world in which desire might be constructed in terms other than those of either superficial romanticism or oppressive bourgeois order. We see Vronsky play to the full the role of the romantic lover, and then witness his transformation into the role of aspiring husband. Neither of these modes of behaviour satisfies Anna's expectations. If she is jealous, and zealous in her refusal of maternity and her commitment to narcissism, such behaviour is derived not from natural causes, but from social reasons – in this case the recognition that only through the maintenance of a highly individualized, romantic relationship can she avoid becoming another wife, perhaps even a betrayed one, in yet another bourgeois marriage.

If there is a message in *Anna Karenina* it is perhaps that domestic life and maternity save women from Anna's hideous fate of morbid jealousy and destructive introspection. Domestic life and maternity protect women against the worthless husband, and good husbands – the Levins of the domestic world – value women as wives and mothers. The message is a somewhat pessimistic one and the various fates of the women in *Anna Karenina* are all, in one way or another, deeply depressing. But what these fates also suggest is Tolstoy's perception of the lives of women. I remarked earlier in this chapter that *Anna Karenina* is deeply ingrained with male guilt: in conclusion I would add the other side to this coin is male fantasy, and fear of the sexual power of women. What we have in the novel is a portrayal in the character of Anna of the sexually powerful, and socially subversive, potential of women and, at the same time, recognition that the way in which this potential is contained and controlled is often damaging and compromising for both women and men. Anna and Vronsky are attracted because of the constraints of bourgeois society (it is part of Anna's initial charm that she radiates a suppressed energy, and a suppressed refusal, of bourgeois order) but that same bourgeois order destroys them. Oblonsky and Dolly are forced into the traditional lies and deceptions of a bourgeois marriage, and even Kitty and Levin – apparently the most suited couple – have to accept the limitations which traditional patterns of sexual differentiation impose. Thus Levin is amazed by his wife's concern with what he sees as domestic trifles, whilst Kitty is upset and disturbed by her husband's absences – both literal and metaphorical – from the family hearth. The world that women construct for their own protection, and the protection of their children, is a world that divides and segregates women and men.

But in this world of disappointments – and ultimately of tragedy – there are no villains or heroes. Men, or a man, do not cause Anna's death, or Dolly's unhappiness, any more than women exhibit jealous or obsessive behaviour solely for innate, unalterable reasons. What is striking about *Anna Karenina* then, and of the figure of Anna in particular, is that the central characters are both highly specific and general: Anna stands for the potential of all women, yet is at the same time the particular wife of a particular Russian bureaucrat. Dolly and Kitty are every wife and mother just as much as they are sisters from an old aristocratic family. What disturbs us about *Anna Karenina* – and clearly what disturbed Tolstoy – is the psychic disorder lurking under the apparent normality of bourgeois society. As in many nineteenth-century novels, Tolstoy employs a sub-plot about a submerged world to emphasize this point. Levin's

Chapter Two

ANNA AND THE OTHERS

A S THE CENTRAL character of *Anna Karenina*, Anna dominates the thoughts of writer and readers. The novel is Anna's history, and only coincidentally that of Kitty and Dolly, Levin, Vronsky, Oblonsky, and Karenin. Yet these characters, like many other minor characters, have a central importance in the novel providing us with an understanding of what Anna is actually like, as a woman, a mother, and a human being. We see Anna primarily through Anna's perceptions and interests, but if we shift the emphasis and look at Anna from the point of view of, for instance, Dolly or Karenin, then we come to see aspects of Anna's interests and character, which suggest a person who is far from sympathetic and even damaging to those with whom she comes into contact. So from one point of view, Anna is the 'natural' heroine of the novel, and a person for whom we are expected to have compassion and pity; from another she is a woman who creates havoc and produces only heartbreak for her intimate associates. These different readings then raise issues about Anna's morality – or lack of it – and the extent to which we can concur with the morality that organizes *Anna Karenina*. One crucial question we need to ask about Anna is this: can we say that it was in some sense her 'fault' that she came to her unhappy end, or was she a victim of unfortunate social circumstances? That question opens up a further area for consideration: in societies in which there are inequalities between the sexes, where women are generally more powerless than men, how do we develop a morality that takes account of these differences, yet does not judge all individuals by some abstract, idealized standard?

Within western feminism, a tradition (although by no means the only tradition) has always asserted that women are 'better' – in a moral sense – than men. The reasons suggested for this moral superiority are many and various; it is explained through women's role as mothers, or through what is supposed to be women's less active, and less aggressive, sexuality or through women's supposed greater capacity for nurturance. All these explanations are varieties of essentialism – women, it is argued, are 'naturally' nicer, kinder, and more careful than men. And it has to be said that this point of view can be supported by some fairly appealing arguments. Women, generally, do not start or go to war and it is this female absence from the universal battlefield that has constituted the organizing basis for such recent campaigns as the British Greenham Common Women's Peace Camp. 'Take the toys from the boys' is one of those resonant, and expressive, slogans that begs for instant agreement and support.

But like many equally appealing slogans it is beset with problems, of which the question of which toys from which boys is only one. There may even be occasions in which women align themselves, however unwillingly, on the same side as some of the boys, and hence find themselves (and here the evidence is substantial) colluding with men and supporting their endeavours against other men, and simultaneously other women. The moral, and political, alliances of the real world shift and change; it is difficult to speak with any finality, in the context of either fiction or fact, of a single moral position for women. Sometimes women (and Anna is no exception here) are victims, at other times they can be instigators of actions that are damaging to others. To read *Anna Karenina* in the hope of finding a female victim of male evil is a task that is doomed to disappointment. From her earliest appearance in the novel Anna is a morally ambivalent character, a character who is far from passive and far from helpless and betrayed.

We first see Anna when she arrives at her brother's home and tries to secure some form of domestic peace between her brother and his wife. She drives from the railway station (and her first encounter with Vronsky) to Oblonsky and Dolly's house and begins immediately to discuss with Dolly Oblonsky's transgressions. So the first significant conversation that Anna has is on the very subject that is to be the theme of the novel – adultery. And the very first thing that Anna says about the subject, and about Oblonsky's affair with his children's governess, is a misrepresentation. Tolstoy has described to us how Oblonsky feels about the situation: sorry for his wife, sorry for the domestic havoc in his home, sorry that his wife found out about the affair, but not particularly sorry about his actions. Yet Anna, apparently a woman of a quick and lively intelligence, describes Oblonsky as 'so humiliated' and 'tormented'. It is hard to imagine Oblonsky in any such state about anything and the conversation between Anna and Dolly on the subject of Oblonsky's emotional state is beset with instances which suggest both Dolly's naïvety and susceptibility and what can only be described as Anna's capacity to deceive, or at the very least to misrepresent, and to do so knowingly and persuasively. Thus Anna, in attempting to persuade Dolly of Oblonsky's contrition, remarks that 'He's in a pitiful state, weighed down by remorse . . .'. Not quite a description which matches the more objective view of Tolstoy:

> Oblonsky was a straightforward man in his dealings with himself. He could not deceive himself into believing that he repented of his conduct. He could not now feel sorry because he, a handsome, susceptible man of thirty-four, was not in love with his wife, who was the mother of five living and two dead children and only a year younger than himself. He only regretted that he had not managed to hide things from her better.[1]

Oblonsky, like Tolstoy, has no hesitation in admitting the emotional reality of the situation; a situation in which men account for their infidelity by reference to the failings and shortcomings of their wives.

But Anna does not attempt to persuade Dolly that it is for Oblonsky to resolve the situation. Instead she explains the situation to Dolly in terms of one of two great myths which women (and men) use to interpret their emotional relationships. The first myth is that of heterosexual romance – a myth, and its implications – which Dolly is now, painfully, confronting in all its shortcomings. As Dolly says to Anna:

> You will hardly believe it, but until this happened I supposed I was the only woman he had ever loved. I lived thinking that for eight years. You see, it not only never entered my head to suspect him of being unfaithful to me – I believed such a thing to be impossible, and then ... imagine what it was like with such ideas to find out all this horror, all this vileness.[2]

So Dolly makes it clear that she had believed in the singular and exclusive nature of the relationship between herself and Oblonsky – and it is a belief that Anna does not question. Indeed, Anna agrees that she fully understands Dolly's feelings. Romance is the perfectly acceptable, and apparently natural, concomitant of bourgeois marriage.

But if that marriage does not quite measure up to the expectations of romance – as that of Dolly and Oblonsky has quite clearly failed to do – then the second myth of bourgeois heterosexuality can be invoked: that whatever men do outside their homes, they see their wives as sacred and value their domestic hearths far above any fleeting attraction. Or, as Anna puts it:

> 'I know the world better than you do,' she said. 'I know how men like Stiva look at things. You speak of his talking about you to her. No such thing. Men may be unfaithful but their homes, their wives are sacred to them. Somehow they still look on these women with contempt and do not let them interfere with their feeling for their family. They draw a sort of line that can't be crossed between them and their families. I do not understand it, but it is so. ... Dolly, listen darling. I saw Stiva when he was in love with you.... You know we have sometimes laughed at him for adding at every turn: "Dolly is a wonderful woman." You always were and still are a goddess in his eyes, and this has not been an infidelity of the heart ...'[3]

The explanation is clearly an effective and a potent one, for after this plea Dolly agrees to feeling better and we see her setting off on the road to some form of *rapprochement* with Oblonsky – a road which is to be no less flawed than the one she has already travelled. Oblonsky is no more faithful, no more careful and conscientious in his dealings with Dolly and his children, than before.

In this conversation, however, Anna has secured for Oblonsky domestic peace, albeit of a fairly shaky and fleeting kind. What she has also done is to outline her thinking, and her unconscious articulation, of how she sees the domestic and romantic life of men and women. She concurs with the idea of romance, and she endorses the view that men, certainly bourgeois men, distinguish between good women (wives and mothers) and bad women (the sexually appealing). That this distinction is made can be demonstrated time and time again in fact and fiction; what is less immediately plausible is Anna's suggestion that men regard their wives as sacred. Here the evidence is more difficult to find, and we enter that realm of imagination and feeling, where people state what they would like to believe rather than what actually is the case. In the case of the specific household of Oblonsky and Dolly, for instance, there is no evidence that Oblonsky regards his wife as either 'sacred' or a 'goddess'. Indeed, as far as we are told he regards her as a rather foolish, and not particularly effective, woman. But Anna presents to Dolly, as *fact*, the idea that for Oblonsky, Dolly is the epitome of all that is most valuable, and venerable, about womanhood.

The belief, internalized by both men and women, that the domestic hearth gives the women who occupy it a sacred quality, is a myth that can be singularly convenient for men, since it allows them to maintain a traditional sexual division of labour, and their exclusive claim to the public world. But it is also a myth that can serve women, in that they can invoke it when they wish to preserve, against male encroachment, specifically female values and interests. Feminism itself has not been slow to use the association of women and children, and women and the household, for the furtherance of female interests. All these different uses of a prevalent domestic ideology can be illustrated in western history. What is less easy to demonstrate is the way in which women imprison themselves in the myths of the 'good woman' and the 'sacred mother', and act out the very divisions that exist between good and bad. Anna and Dolly are cases in point. Dolly admits to romance, she is easily convinced by Anna's account of her sacred status and it takes her months and years to unlearn and forget this second misleading interpretation of her relationship with Oblonsky. In Dolly we can see the gradual disillusionment of a woman who entered marriage valuing romance and who only gradually comes to see her husband as a creature of reality rather than fiction.

With Anna there is a more complicated pattern; in conversation with Dolly Anna reveals not only her capacity to deceive others, but also both her ability to deceive herself and her own collusion with those fictions she uses to persuade Dolly to forgive Oblonsky. Anna, we learn from this conversation, believes in romance. But what we also learn is that Anna believes that it is difficult for men, for conventional bourgeois men, to respect women with whom they have unconventional relationships. The conversation thus predicts and pre-figures many of the tensions that are later to occur between Anna and Vronsky. Anna is forced to go on maintaining and invoking romance, while unable to forget her suspicion that Vronsky regards her as 'merely' a sexual object. Thus, the two most significant conversations that Dolly and Anna have reveal the values of these two characters, and the elaboration of the characters' own interpretations of these values. In the first conversation, Anna persuades Dolly that she should remain in a conventional marriage – and should do so because what men value is the home and their children rather than romance. In the second conversation (which takes place when Dolly visits Anna at Vronsky's country estate) Anna attempts to persuade Dolly of the continuing vitality of her romance with Vronsky. In this attempt Anna is singularly unsuccessful. Dolly is convinced of Vronsky's feeling for Anna, but she is not persuaded that sexual attraction will sustain their relationship.

So the conversation between Dolly and Anna which occurs at the beginning of the novel reveals the essentially traditional and conventional views that Anna has about relationships between men and women. What gives this first conversation its overtone of tragedy is that Anna is endorsing precisely those views about men and women which, because Vronsky also believes them, are to lead to the eventually tragic and bitter end of their relationship. Anna not only believes in romance, she also apparently believes in that dichotomy between 'good' and 'bad' women of which she is so enthusiastic an exponent in her first conversation with Dolly. The final chapters of *Anna Karenina* are thus replete with Anna's own crippling self-evaluation as a 'bad' woman. She begs reassurance from Vronsky that this is not the case – but Vronsky cannot reassure her since he finds such behaviour inexplicable, and has no reassurance to offer a woman who has refused his best efforts to convert her into a 'good' woman – that is Mrs Vronsky, and the mother of the Vronsky children. Vronsky becomes, in Anna's eyes, yet another man – like Karenin and Oblonsky in their different ways – who cannot appreciate or value a woman's love.

This interpretation of Vronsky, the belief that he had forever placed love and romance at the centre of his existence, is perhaps Anna's most damaging and dangerous mistake. Such, however, was the case and Tolstoy tells us that for Anna:

> ... Vronsky, with all his habits, ideas, desires – his whole spiritual and physical temperament – could be summed up in one thing – love for women, and this love, which she felt ought to be concentrated on her, was diminishing. Therefore, she reasoned, he must have transferred part of it to other women, or to another woman, and she was jealous.[4]

But it is difficult to concur with this judgement of Vronsky. Indeed, Vronsky, although deeply in love with Anna and apparently committed to their relationship, never ceases to be a male, Russian aristocrat. As such, he is interested in his career, his male friends, and his place in society. Whatever happiness he can find with Anna, however intense that happiness, cannot satisfy all his needs for interest and variety. Above all, Vronsky is conventional – conventional in his attitude to Anna, to the world, and to social relations.

Anna and the Others

A contributory element in Anna's tragedy therefore is that she misreads the subject of her passionate love. A woman capable of powerful emotions, and of producing powerful emotional reactions in others, she is also a victim of that same emotional intensity. In examining the construction of Anna's character and personality a number of disparate elements emerge: a fiercely passionate nature, an ability to control aspects of the social world (witness her initial manipulation of the grieved and hurt Dolly), an adoring mother, and an accomplished social personality are all elements which vie for centrality but are also accompanied by fatal misinterpretations of the motives and expectations of others. The questions about Anna that remain intriguing and perplexing are thus questions about the origin of her needs and her manifest failure to construct a world capable of meeting them. Anna can be read as a victim of the ideology of romance and the social powerlessness of women. Indeed, her history and her behaviour support this argument. But to make Anna a victim ignores her capacity to manipulate and control others, and it ignores the more general theoretical issue of the complex ways in which emotional needs and desires are at one and the same time developed, articulated, and denied within a single society.

An examination of how Anna acts with, and towards, other people leaves the powerful impression that she does not, in Tolstoy's terms, behave very well. Her initial entry into the action of the novel is the conversational deceit of Dolly; her second appearance reveals a display of her sexual power at the ball which she, Vronsky, and Kitty attend. Anna knows full well that Kitty is strongly attracted to Vronsky, and that Kitty as a young, unmarried girl has no access to the language and behaviour of sexuality which Anna, as a married woman, can command. Nevertheless, knowing all this, Anna displays her sexual attractiveness and power. She does not dress simply for a ball, or behave merely appropriately, she dresses to inspire desire and to claim for herself sexual appeal and erotic centrality. Provoked by the presence of Vronsky Anna becomes, as Kitty sees, 'intoxicated with the admiration she had aroused'. Kitty's previous admiration, almost infatuation, with Anna then shifts rapidly from pleasure at the sight of her loveliness and grace to something approaching fear at the feelings Anna can invoke, particularly as Vronsky is clearly captivated by her behaviour at the ball.

Thus what had begun, for Kitty, as an evening full of happiness and rich possibility, ends sadly and with disappointment. Anna's decision to leave the ball early serves merely to reinforce the impression of her narcissism. Having accomplished disturbance, having made, as it were, her statement about herself, she leaves. The ball is not merely a social occasion in which Anna participates with others, but an opportunity for the demonstration of Anna's sexual potential. The shift is important, for what we learn from her behaviour is that Anna is not only capable of personal manipulation but also of imposing her mark on social events. This woman, then, is not just effective in her dealings with single others, she is also potentially powerful in her effect on groups. But is is in these situations, the situations that involve more than one person, that we also see Anna's – and women's – weakness. The weakness is that whatever the personal strength and power of women they have fewer resources than men at their disposal for the manipulation and control of the social world. So at an occasion which is essentially about play and acting-out (that is, a society ball) there is an arena for the demonstration of women's power. But in the world of politics, of the institutions of the law and the state and the market place, women are mostly denied access to power and control.

And access – or lack of access – to the control of the public world is what makes Anna so dependent on Karenin, and so deeply trapped in a situation from which there appears to be no escape. Anna, like all the wives in the novel, needs a husband to act for her in the social world. Levin does this for Kitty, Oblonsky does it (albeit most unsatisfactorily) for Dolly and Karenin does it (both before and after the rupture in their marriage) for Anna. Whatever the powers of women in the home or ballroom, they have no real access or control of the public world. When Anna wishes to obtain a divorce from Karenin she cannot do so without male permission and male intervention. When Anna wants access to her son, she cannot obtain this without the same male approval. Equally, when Kitty and Dolly need to make social arrangements they have to call on male assistance and agreement. In the case of Dolly this makes her the victim of Oblonsky's laziness and casual fecklessness, and although we never see it we might conjecture that Kitty will become the victim (like Mrs Tolstoy) of her husband's high-minded asceticism and puritanism. All these examples, Kitty, Dolly, and Anna herself, could be replicated a hundred times in fiction and countless millions of times in reality.

But the point here is less to establish that women are socially and publicly less powerful than men (for that has been documented and described widely elsewhere) than to suggest that part of the dilemma that confronts Anna is this very issue of personal power and social powerlessness. Thus, for women, sexuality and sexual power become weapons, and they do so because there are no, or few, other weapons at their command. Anna's sexual power, and her ability to radiate emotional and sexual vitality, is at least as much socially created as it is naturally given. What is naturally given, what is, as far as we know, unique to Anna, is a physical beauty and charm which is endorsed by a particular society. But what Anna shares with many other women is a recognition that all human beings have the potential to be effective in the world, although it is a potential that is, in women, given few opportunities for development and articulation. Anna is an intelligent, worldly woman, who reads and supports the principle of the education of women. (Indeed she is angry with Vronsky when he belittles the attempts of a friend of hers to educate herself.) Yet she has little to do that constitutes engaging or serious employment. This is not to imply that had the Open University been available to Anna Karenina she would not have embarked on her affair with Vronsky, but it is to suggest that human satisfaction and happiness – and Anna's was no exception – needs a means, a structure through which to organize itself.

Unfortunately for Anna, and other women like her, there was little for them to do which could provide the promise of emotional and intellectual rewards. Tolstoy's answer to the problem of the intelligent bourgeois and aristocratic woman is a concentration on and absorption with the household and family. The patriarchal answer that Tolstoy advocated for his own wife, and his own life, is also the answer that he offers in fiction. Dolly and Kitty are 'saved' from narcissism, from vanity and marital deceit and infidelity by their domestic concerns. So too is Natasha in *War and Peace*. The young, vital heroine who so captivates Prince Andrew, and Pierre, is transposed by the patriarchal hand of the author into the nagging wife and mother. Her sexual vitality is directed solely towards maternity, and her intelligence and interest in the public world towards the concerns of the family and her household. But Anna, unlike Natasha (who parallels Anna in that she is almost, but not quite, guilty of sexual transgression), is not allowed this salvation. Anna is not permitted to marry happily and to settle into the comfortable (and convenient) role of wife and mother.

And it is not, in a way, that the author does not give her every opportunity. Tolstoy provides Anna with a child whom she adores, a faithful and reasonably attentive husband, and a secure social position. But this provision of all that should satisfy Anna only serves to sharpen the morality, and the moral judgement, that lurks in *Anna Karenina*. Is, then, Tolstoy asking us to believe that he did everything that he could for Anna, but she still let him down? If so, her death is her fault, and the explanation and responsibility for Anna's tragedy lies solely and entirely with Anna herself. Anna is not the victim of social pressures and social arrangements but, literally, the guilty party in a wrecked marriage and several wrecked lives. Even if Anna is not guilty, in the strict ethical sense of having deliberately chosen between good and bad and in the full knowledge of both, she still emerges as guilty in the wider sense of a person who was unable to control and discipline her passions and her inclinations. The case for Tolstoy, and against Anna, is not insubstantial. Anna is not particularly sympathetic in her dealings with others – she deceives Dolly, she wounds Kitty, and she deserts Seriozha. It is impossible to argue that she deceives Karenin, indeed she chooses revelation rather than deceit. But she does demonstrate contempt and scorn for him, and a carelessness bordering on neglect for her daughter by Vronsky.

Yet however great the damage done to these characters by Anna, it is Vronsky who is most obviously wounded, apparently fatally, by Anna. As already suggested, Anna fatally misinterprets Vronsky by believing him to be a man whose life is dominated by attentions to women. What was, in fact, apparent before his meeting with Anna was that Vronsky was in no sense preoccupied with women. Women had a clearly defined and compartmentalized place in his world, but they were only part of it. A large part of the rest of Vronsky's world was filled by his concern with his career, his estate, and his relationship with his fellow officers. As Tolstoy remarks of Vronsky, he was 'a man who hated disorder'. Moreover, Vronsky is happiest when he can live his life by a code of principles:

> This code of principles covered only a very small circle of contingencies, but in return the principles were never obscure, and Vronsky, as he never went outside that circle, had never had a moment's hesitation about doing what he ought to do.... These principles might be irrational and not good, but they were absolute and in complying with them Vronsky felt at ease and could hold his head high. Only quite lately, in regard to his relations with Anna, Vronsky had begun to feel that his code did not quite meet all circumstances and that the future presented doubts and difficulties for which he could find no guiding thread.[5]

Affairs, such as Vronsky's with Anna, should be organized, according to the aristocratic world from which Vronsky came, by tact, discretion, and a respect for the status quo. Aristocrats of both sexes could have extramarital affairs, so much was tolerated if not condoned, but what these affairs were not expected to do was disturb the order of life, the concerns and interests of the family, the estate and the nation (or, as Engels said, the family, private property, and the state). The problem about the relationship between Anna and Vronsky is that it seems to be taking on what Vronsky's mother perceived as a

'Werther-like' passion.

These reservations turn out to be, of course, entirely accurate. Vronsky's code of behaviour, and his very capacity to understand the emotional world in general and Anna's in particular, is deeply inadequate when it comes to dealing with the implications and repercussions of his affair with Anna. Two problems are prominent: the impossibility of compartment-alizing Anna and Anna's refusal to be turned into a respectable woman. In the passages of the novel that discuss Vronsky's reaction when Anna reveals she is expecting his child, Vronsky's mixed feelings, and inadequate understanding, become most marked. Vronsky, we are told, believed that Anna deserved all his respect and loyalty: 'She was an honourable woman who had bestowed her love upon him, and he loved her, therefore she was in his eyes a woman who had a right to the same, or even more respect than a lawful wife.' Vronsky's attitude to Karenin is that he is a 'superfluous person and a hindrance', whom Vronsky is quite prepared to meet in a duel but is otherwise inclined to ignore. So far so good: Vronsky knows what he thinks about Anna – and where she belongs in his emotional hierarchy and pattern – and where Karenin belongs.

Then the pregnancy is revealed. This does not, at first, present problems to Vronsky since he is perfectly aware that the aristocratic code (to which he assumes Karenin conforms) could accommodate the birth of a child to Anna. The child would simply be regarded as Karenin's (and indeed the child does take Karenin's name) and social paternity would be allowed precedence over physical paternity. Again, there is an order and a set of rules for dealing with these events – an order which Vronsky and the Karenins both know and have seen implemented in practice. But emotions other than his love for Anna are also part of Vronsky's life, and the passion for Anna, whilst sincere and all-consuming, has to co-exist with Vronsky's personal ambitions, his respect for order, and his delight in male camaraderie. Vronsky is thus confronted with a situation which he finds frightening because of its vagueness. He muses to himself:

> If I urged her to leave her husband, that must mean uniting her
> life with mine. Am I prepared for that? How can I take her away
> now, when I have no money? Supposing I could arrange.... But
> how could I go away with her while I'm in the service? If I say
> that – I must be ready to do it, that is, I ought to have the money
> and retire from the army.[6]

In the event, Vronsky does leave the army, but only after some
considerable struggles with himself, and with grave doubts
about the advisability of his actions. We are left in no doubt that
the decision is a tussle: Vronsky has to admit to himself that he
has ambitions for his army life. Thus we learn that 'Ambition
was the old dream of his youth and boyhood, a dream he did not
confess even to himself, though it was so strong that even now
this passion was doing battle with his love.' Although Vronsky
has wished to give the world the impression that he is a
dashing, insouciant person, above the bourgeois demands and
imperatives of application to his career, he is in fact deeply
committed to the army, and his self-advancement. The
apparently confident, careless, and independent young officer,
admired by all for his panache and his splendid vigour, is also
the much more mundane young officer with a serious interest
in his career.

Vronsky is not quite so different from Karenin as a first
reading might suggest. Indeed, Anna's dream about her
husband and her lover unites them in a way which is
particularly revealing about her perception, albeit a subcon-
scious one, of the characteristics that the two men share. When
Anna dreams of Vronsky and Karenin she dreams that both are
showering affection on her, and that she is quite content to
receive this joint tribute. Vronsky, Karenin, and Anna are
united in an apparently happy and contented threesome – a
unity that is broken only when Anna awakes and relives her
dream not as a happy memory but as a terrifying nightmare.
For Anna the dream is frightening, but for readers of *Anna
Karenina* it is fascinating for the questions it suggests about
Anna's relations to Vronsky and Karenin and, not least, to her
own needs and desires. In the dream Vronsky and Karenin are
brought closer together than they are ever to be in real life, even

though such unity is not altogether far-fetched or merely a matter of the imagination, given what can be deduced about the similarities between them. Both are orderly, ambitious, and hard working men – these bourgeois values may be a little disguised in Vronsky but it takes only the slightest hint of social or personal disorder to reveal them. Both men are deeply committed to Anna, and to the notion of singularity and exclusivity in any relationship with her. Anna, it would seem, has chosen for her lover a man who may resemble her husband more than she is prepared to admit or accept.

But since Vronsky does share so much with Karenin it also becomes more necessary, in an emotional sense, for Anna to distinguish him from Karenin. If Vronsky is the same as, or very similar to, Karenin then Anna's very selfhood and identity are threatened, since she has made a commitment which is, in effect, emotionally pointless. She has chosen not a person who can liberate her from the strictures and constraints of marriage but a person who is disposed to replicate these constraints. Marriage and emotional life with Vronsky will become not the satisfying and emancipating experience that Anna hopes for but another version of an unwilling, coerced, and unhappy life. Anna's refusal to come to terms with her situation after the rupture with Karenin and her aggressive disinterest in a divorce begins to fall into a pattern in which the social pressures that affect all men and all women can be discerned. In summary, what can be seen is this: that Anna perceives, albeit unwillingly and grudgingly, the similarities both between Vronsky and Karenin and between her situation when married to either. Having made this observation it becomes essential for Anna to maintain the romance and the emotional singularity of her relationship with Vronsky. The romance cannot be maintained for two main reasons: Vronsky's life includes other interests besides his relationship with Anna, and Anna's demands for romance and almost hourly romantic, and sexual, confirmation are impossible for Vronsky to meet. Anna is then left isolated, no longer able to disguise an unpalatable truth; there is more in common between Vronsky and Karenin than appearances suggest; the Vronsky who was once the object of her romantic and all-consuming passions was more a creature of her own projected needs and desires than he was ever a creature of flesh. Anna, in effect, created a romantic object out of her own needs, but could not control or construct the object in ways that satisfied her desires.

The idea that Vronsky, of all the characters in *Anna Karenina*, is the person most damaged by Anna's fantasies needs to be explored in greater depth. Vronsky's appeal to Anna, given his physical charm and grace, is considerable, but out of this appeal – an appeal much enhanced by the less immediately attractive figure of Karenin – Anna constructs the mythical Vronsky. That Vronsky could never realize her expectations makes him deeply vulnerable to Anna's needs, as Anna herself is vulnerable to the force of her own unmet desires. It is not that Anna 'deliberately' damages Vronsky, or that there is an intent on her part to destroy him. It is much more that Anna, denied erotic and emotional satisfaction with Karenin, is unable to limit her capacity to create for herself the ideal person to complement her needs. The story of the relationship has no obvious villain. There is certainly, in a literal sense, an obvious victim (in that Anna ends her life beneath the wheels of a train) but there are other victims as well.

The history of Anna and Vronsky is not, evidently, a happy one. But in all her relationships with others Anna unfailingly disappoints and/or injures. Inevitably, we look for some explanation for this general, and massive disappointment. A beautiful woman, a successful husband and lover, and an adored son are brought to misery by forces which none escape, let alone control. What kinds of pressures and needs create this situation? Which characters are to blame? Or is nobody, and everybody, responsible for the heroine's death and the ruin of the lives of the central characters? At this point, arguments can be introduced about personal responsibility and social pressures – arguments that remove some of the burden of guilt from the shoulders of individual characters. Mitigating circumstances must be introduced to save Anna from moral condemnation as 'bad', or Vronsky as 'callous' – labels that are all too easily applied to others in similar circumstances. After all, the mother, a married woman, who deliberately chooses an adulterous relationship rather than her maternal responsibilities would still today be labelled as a deviant and 'unnatural' woman, just as a man who breaks up a home and a family would be deemed immoral, and accountable for the woman's fate. The characters of Anna and Vronsky, Seriozha and Karenin, are characters of fiction, but the situation of this quartet (of natural parents, children, lovers, and putative step-parent) is a commonplace of western life.

Explanations about the breakdown of family life, and socially unacceptable behaviour in personal and social relations, inevitably reveal deep political and moral differences between individuals and factions. One school of thought (which might coincide with the political Right) would condemn Anna and Vronsky (and their successors in suburbia) for their 'immorality' and carelessness in personal behaviour. No doubt Mrs Whitehouse and Jerry Falwell could thunder forth about Anna and Vronsky with as much enthusiasm as they thunder forth about the later exploits of both fictional and factual characters. In terms of existing social and institutional practice in the west, it is at least conceivable that Anna (although she could nowadays obtain a relatively straightforward divorce from Karenin) would not be given custody of Seriozha and that Vronsky would certainly be expected to maintain Anna. Anna, as much in the 1980s as in the 1880s, would still be subject to the inequalities and biases of the law. But in the 1980s there would also be a strongly voiced alternative interpretation of Anna's situation, an interpretation which would stress that Anna was not, in any significant sense, to 'blame' for the nature and circumstances of her death and that the real villains of the story are not individuals but socially diffuse characters called patriarchy and bourgeois repression. These all-encompassing and virtually universally-present gremlins make people behave in ways that are damaging, unattractive, and even tragic in their results. Individual moral responsibility is therefore removed, and Anna, Vronsky and the others become the hapless subjects of patriarchy and the industries of romance and eroticism. The chief theoretical problem with this explanation is that a general phenomenon does not produce general results. Kitty and Dolly (despite the disappointments and tribulations of their lives and their relationships with men) do not end up dead, nor are their families split apart by dissent and disaster. Equally, the equivalents of Kitty and Dolly in real life do not take lovers, get divorced or embark on any other form of unconventional social behaviour. We all live under (or with) patriarchy, and bourgeois repression, but we do not all make of those circumstances the same personal history.

What, then, distinguishes Anna from the rest? It is apparent from Tolstoy's account of their lives and hopes that Kitty and Dolly entertained the same romantic hopes of marriage as Anna. Like Anna, Kitty and Dolly faced the mundane disappointments of erotic hopes that were located in daily domestic life. Yet they manage to survive these disappointments. Levin, the man whose expectations of women are arguably the highest, also manages to survive what he discovers as the inadequacies of the object of his desire. In all these cases, idealized desire and romantic disappointments are brought low by the commonplace interventions of the household and everyday life, but these very interventions provide for the characters a new *raison d'être*, a new form of defining their existence. For example, Oblonsky is certainly a deep disappointment to Dolly, but she has five children to rear and two households to maintain and organize into some semblance of order. Such preoccupations do not satisfy Anna. Maternity, as we have seen, is no consolation to her, and she is content – when living with Karenin as much as with Vronsky – to leave the detailed arrangements of her household to paid staff. Patently, this is not a woman who is going to devote attention to household detail and the minute and detailed supervision of living arrangements. Indeed, in both households (Anna and Karenin and Anna and Vronsky) it is the man who takes on the responsibility for domestic care. Both men (and this is perhaps part of Anna's nightmare) turn out to be deeply interested in their domestic worlds. Both men, apparently, wish to translate passion into bourgeois order.

But such transformations strike at the heart of Anna's particularity – her narcissism and her powerful eroticism. The two are so closely related that it is almost impossible to separate them: for Anna her identity is her sexual power, and when thwarted in that expression she becomes either dissatisfied (as with Karenin) or deeply unhappy (as with Vronsky). The elements of Anna's narcissism are many and various. Of all the female characters in the novel she is the most concerned with dress, of all the mothers in the novel she is the most articulate on the subject of her child's desirability and emotional potency and of all the wives in the novel she is the least able to surrender her sense of self to an identity based on the household, and hence on the rule and authority of its patriarchal head. Paradoxically, this apparent rejection of patriarchy in the general sense also makes Anna the most vulnerable to men (and a man) in the particular. Neither Kitty nor Dolly regards their husbands with indifference, but Anna regards both Vronsky and Karenin with an intensity which suggests an inordinate, and perhaps exceptional, need for male confirmation and erotic satisfaction. Only Vronsky, it becomes tragically apparent in the concluding pages of the novel, can satisfy Anna's sense of herself and only Vronsky can reassure Anna that she has made the correct choices, and is affirmed in these choices by the devotion of her lover.

Unhappily her lover cannot meet these demands. Indeed, if we read Anna, not as a real person but as a metaphor for female desire – or a male perception of the possible strength and passion of female desire – then it is apparent that no man could meet the needs of this passion. Removing Anna and Vronsky, and discussing not individuals but general types, we find in *Anna Karenina* a vision of relations between the sexes in which the ability of women to create male desire is far greater than the capacity of men to satisfy either their own desires or those of women. The conventional suggestion that men are perceived as sexually active and women as sexually passive is therefore reversed in *Anna Karenina*. In Tolstoy's imaginative world women create desire – it is the function of men to attempt to satisfy it. But – and it is a crucial and central part of the creation of desire in western culture – the very erotic power of women is actually brought into existence by the mechanism which society, and largely men as the organizers of public social life, create to contain and organize the sexuality of women. Because Anna is denied the possibility of fulfilling her sexual and emotional needs in her relationship with Karenin, her vitality expresses itself in a forced liveliness, in excessive personal narcissism, and in an almost incestuous passion for her son. Karenin's denial of Anna's needs, far from disciplining them, or turning them into avenues which he would regard as acceptable, merely serves to increase them. Vronsky, in his turn, is to do exactly the same thing. At first entranced by Anna, and delighted to enter into such an erotically-charged relationship, he rapidly finds that he cannot control the force of Anna's desires. His expectations were that he would seduce Anna, and that without too much ado she would rapidly organize her sexuality into the acceptable form of sexually compliant woman and willing mother. Against all his conventional expectations, Anna refuses to play either part. She will not join the sisterhood of wives, and she prevents Vronsky from entering the brotherhood of husbands.

The isolation, both personal and social, to which Anna condemns herself is also an isolation which in part derives from social circumstances. Divorce would not have been easy for Anna, and acceptance by certain circles of aristocratic Russia would never have been given. But even if these circumstances were different it would be difficult to imagine Vronsky and Anna settling down to become another married couple. The very romance and ardour which fuelled and instigated their relationship becomes the means through which it is condemned. The ideology of romance, the language in which heterosexual relationships are created and organized, is thus the language which can condemn individuals to an endless pursuit of redundant passions. Tolstoy does not allow Anna to recognize and accept other possibilities than her relationship with Vronsky, but he does suggest to his readers, through the account of the personal history of Levin, that the recognition of the inevitable disappointment of sexual desire is part of a necessary accommodation to the world which has to be made. To quote Freud again: 'We must reckon with the possibility that something in the nature of the sexual instinct is unfavourable to the realisation of complete satisfaction.'

But if the sexual instinct cannot be completely satisfied then that makes that instinct unstable and potentially disruptive. Which is, of course, exactly what Anna is – unstable, disruptive, and demonstrably capable of producing havoc in the lives of all around her. Her sexuality is so potent that no individual can match it: thus, when she dreams of her husband and lover together she may be acknowledging not only that they are much the same person, but that she needs both of them. Unfortunately for Anna, women in western culture are not expected to have either sexual needs, let alone needs that can only be satisfied by multiple relationships. Equally unfortunately for Anna, this cultural expectation is universally applied to individual cases. It is not that Anna alone experiences jealousy or desires a single, all-encompassing love – Vronsky and Karenin expect this as well and attempt to channel Anna's desire in culturally appropriate ways. Both men are as jealous of Anna as Anna is later to be of Vronsky, and both are articulate exponents of their views about what Anna ought to do. Yet, as Anna realizes, conceding to either Vronsky or Karenin involves conceding to the moral order and imperatives of patriarchy: her choice is to become either a mistress or a guilty wife, and her dream of living her love in freedom is limited by these constraints.

The course that Anna chooses – that of becoming publicly known as Vronsky's mistress – alienates her from respectable society and ensures her estrangement from Seriozha. From the first, Vronsky and Anna find the mere presence of Seriozha almost impossible to deal with:

> The child's presence invariably called up in Vronsky that strange feeling of inexplicable revulsion which he had experienced of late. The child's presence called up both in Vronsky and in Anna a feeling akin to that of a sailor who can see by the compass that the direction in which he is swiftly sailing is wide of the proper course, but is powerless to stop. Every moment takes him farther

and farther astray, and to admit to himself that he is off his course is the same as admitting final disaster.

This child, with his innocent outlook upon life, was the compass which showed them the degree to which they had departed from what they knew but did not want to know.[7]

Seriozha stands in relationship to Vronsky in the classically difficult and fraught position of step-child, a position that is generally documented in fiction as unhappy and potentially damaging. Karenin's son constantly reminds Vronsky, and Anna, of the relationship between Anna and Karenin which both would very much prefer to forget. But Seriozha, as Tolstoy is suggesting, does something more than that: he reminds Vronsky and Anna of the moral dimensions and implications of their actions and he is a living testimony to the existence of a form of human love and affection that is at least as strong as that of adult sexuality and adult sexual relationships, that of parenthood and, in this particular case, of maternal love. In the triangle between Anna, Seriozha, and Vronsky, it is Seriozha who is the apparent loser. Anna chooses Vronsky rather than Seriozha but she never abandons her commitment to her son, nor does the strength of her love for him weaken.

When Anna dreams about a peasant and a bar of iron she provides us with an insight into her subjective experience of living in a society which both sanctions and encourages heterosexual desire and yet denies and suppresses it. The iron cage, those social laws about individual emotional and sexual behaviour, make it impossible for Anna to love Vronsky in anything approaching the freedom of which she dreamt, to respect the integrity of Karenin or – perhaps most importantly – to maintain the relationship with her son. The choices facing Anna are limited and circumscribed, as are the choices which, in their turn, are given to the other central characters. But as adults these individuals all have the power of choice. The poignancy of Seriozha's situation, and the power of Tolstoy's metaphor about Seriozha's role as a moral compass, is that as a child Seriozha had no choice, no say, in the lives of the adults who surrounded him. The rules of patriarchal order are such that Seriozha has to remain with his father, the rules of this

order are also such that Seriozha is forbidden to remember Anna
or mourn her loss. He is told by Karenin, and the male world of
tutor, school and peers, that grown men do not indulge in
desperate longings for their mother, let alone give vent to their
feelings in tears. Affectivity in men is proscribed, yet men are
expected – indeed encouraged – to be passionate about women
and to value them. But they are only allowed to do this if they
agree to pay the price of loving women as adult men – that is as
people who expect women to fulfil given roles and accept the
double burden of male need and male control. The 'pure' love
of women for children is, therefore, both an accurate and a
misleading compass, for at the same time as the existence of
Seriozha confronts Anna and Vronsky with the implications of
their actions for others, and especially innocent others (and is
therefore a moral touchstone), it is also at best a temporary
guide. Seriozha is a child when he so disturbs Anna and
Vronsky, but he is also going to grow up as a man.

And this recognition that the innocence of childhood – and
the moral force of innocence – is undermined by the inevitable
changes of time and adult life, is also part of Anna's perception.
Agonizing though the scenes with Seriozha are, Tolstoy forces
us to confront the limits of maternal affection and
commitment. Dolly and Kitty find enormous pleasure in their
relationships with their children, and yet in Dolly's nursery, in
the scenes of ordinary fights and squabbles between the
children, Tolstoy tells us that however powerful maternal love
is, it cannot produce ideal children nor can it be a substitute for
adult affection. That it can be a compensation, and indeed a
source of pleasure, there is no doubt. But the belief that it can
ever be a completely satisfying relationship for either party is
one that Tolstoy disputes. In those moments when Anna
considers motherhood, and her role as a mother, in contrast to
her relationships with others, Tolstoy writes with irony of the
self-delusion that Anna has attempted in her attitude to
Seriozha:

> The thought of her son suddenly aroused Anna from the
> helpless condition in which she found herself. She remembered

the partly sincere, though greatly exaggerated role of the mother living for her child, which she had assumed during the last few years, and she felt with joy that in the plight in which she was now she had a support, quite apart from her relation to her husband or to Vronsky. This support was her son.[8]

Inevitably, Seriozha, a child of five, cannot offer his mother anything approaching support. All he can offer, in the unspoken communication between them, is reproach for what is, from Seriozha's point of view, Anna's betrayal and rejection of him. Yet again, Anna's needs have the effect of alienating her from the people she most loves. Vronsky becomes cold and hostile in response to her jealousy, we see Seriozha becoming as emotionally unresponsive and inexpressive as his father in response to Anna's departure. Dreams and memories of his mother become 'shameful and fit only for girls', and:

> ... in order not to blame his father, with whom he lived and upon whom he depended, and above all not to give way to the emotion which he considered so degrading, Seriozha tried not to look at this uncle, who had come to upset his peace of mind, and not to think of what he reminded him of.[9]

Seriozha is involved, like Vronsky, in an intense and emotionally charged relationship with Anna, and becomes – again like Vronsky – separated from her. Even more strikingly, Seriozha and Vronsky both become similar to Karenin in their attitude to Anna, namely cold and uncommunicative. The passions and delights that Anna could inspire in them all are brought to nought – indeed, worse, are brought to disaster – by the intensity of those passions.

If there is any single feature of Anna's relations with others that we can observe in *Anna Karenina* it is, surely, that her needs and desires are such that they cannot be contained or expressed within conventional relations and roles. Thus Anna's sexual desire for Vronsky is fatally pre-ordained to express itself as 'love' but as love that carries social expectations and assumptions that cannot, in this case, be fulfilled. Vronsky comes to recognize his own limitations, but his recognition is a perception of his ordinary human limitations. Anna's

perception of Vronsky is, finally, more radical and more tragic
in its consequences. It is Anna's recognition that the failure of
her relationship with Vronsky (like the failure of the
relationship with Karenin and Seriozha) has less to do with
these individuals and more to do with those social sanctions
that inhibit the fulfilment of her love. Nobody, man, woman,
or child, can satisfy Anna's needs, since her needs are those
absolute human needs for reassurance and self-definition.
Nothing, in a society that separates men and women, children
and adults, is arranged to maximize the possible fulfilment of
those needs: Karenin cannot meet Anna's needs because he is a
man trained to work, think, and respond in a way hostile to
affectivity. Like the Prussian husband in Fontane's *Effi Briest*,
Karenin is guided by those apparently objective rules of conduct
and behaviour which offer little place for individual choice and
change. But Anna's needs transform Vronsky into a similar
figure. Vronsky does not become a model bureaucrat but he
does become a man who in the face of female, and indeed
human, desires adopts the same protective appearance of
objective rationality and common sense as Karenin. Knowing
full well that Anna's coldness and hostility to him disguises a
desperate need, Vronsky chooses to interpret Anna's behaviour
at face value. Thus, after a quarrel, Vronsky leaves the house
but on his return fails to reassure Anna:

> In the evening she heard his carriage stop, heard him ring, heard
> his steps and his voice talking to the maid. He had taken the
> maid's word, did not care to find out more, and went to his
> room. So all was over! [10]

A few pages later all is, literally, over and Anna lies dead,
leaving a trail of unhappy, indeed shattered, lives behind her.
At almost the same time as Anna flings herself under a train,
Kitty is happily and busily employed in the country with her
husband and her young baby son. Why, then, is Anna dead, and
Kitty so cheerfully alive?

Chapter Three

OTHER WOMEN

WHEN TOLSTOY leaves Levin and Kitty gazing at the stars at the conclusion of *Anna Karenina* he also leaves Anna dead, Vronsky broken-heated, and Oblonsky and Dolly locked into a marriage that is demeaning and riddled with mutual deceit and misery. Even the apparent happiness and contentment of Levin and Kitty is qualified. Levin has had to accommodate himself to what he regards as the triviality of his wife's interests, and Kitty is already beginning to follow the path of Natasha in *War and Peace* towards a total preoccupation with her household and her children. The lack of variety in the emotional fate of these characters is a striking aspect of Tolstoy's perception of the human condition. For men, the path is either absorption (as for Levin and Karenin) in work and the public domain, or a preoccupation with self-indulgence and thoughtless hedonism, and here Oblonsky is the representative case. For women, the choices are even narrower: be a good and dutiful wife and mother, or face the fate of Anna, or, in a less extreme case, the life of the outcast mistress of Levin's brother.

The moral and the social fates for women proposed by Tolstoy are indeed limited: a life of domestic respectability in which sexual attraction and activity are denied, or a life of explicit sexual association which carries the cost of exclusion from respectable society. The subtitle of *Anna Karenina* could almost be: What Can Women Do About Sex? The answer, if they wish to avoid the fate of Anna, is to locate sexual activity only and firmly within the legitimate context of heterosexual monogamy. Sexual relations between men and women are virtually exclusively related to the procreation of children. Sexual pleasure is regarded with great suspicion, as the consequences of its appeal are only too likely to be disruptive for all concerned. The moral message of *Anna Karenina* is therefore simple: sex is dangerous and best avoided except for the specific purpose of reproduction. Having reproduced, the sexes can then develop their own, somewhat disparate lives; women have children to occupy their energies and men have heirs to whom they can bequeath their labour and social position.

Anna rejects this model of appropriate behaviour. In doing so she gives to the lives of Dolly and Kitty an apparently reassuring respectability and purpose. At first glance, it is impossible not to choose to be Dolly or Kitty rather than Anna. Whatever their problems and difficulties Dolly and Kitty leave the novel as they enter it – socially acceptable and alive. But at a second glance the situations of Dolly and Kitty could be read as tormented and as unsatisfactory as that of Anna. The difference is that their difficulties do not express themselves in the same dramatic way as those of Anna. Neither is driven to suicide, and neither leaves behind children and men who are shattered by their loss. Yet what they have to endure, or at least live out, is a version of female experience that is in its way as constricting and as damaging as Anna's anguished world. Both Dolly and Kitty spend their lives in domestic seclusion and preoccupation. Their cares are essentially related to events in their husbands' lives and their autonomy limited to the most superficial and trivial choices of dress and private housekeeping. And the lives of Dolly and Kitty, however respectable and well regarded, are not likely to change. They will grow old as their mothers grew old – making jam in the summer and fretting about the health and welfare of their children and husbands. Ordinary human concerns will dominate their lives, as they dominate the lives of the majority of every population of every society, and autonomous actions or interests will largely be absent or limited. As relatively prosperous people, Kitty and Dolly are unlikely to experience material deprivation and misery (although what happens to them after 1917 must remain a matter of speculation) and thus will be envied by many of their immediate contemporaries. They are privileged women who can expect to live to old age and bring up their children with the same expectation.

But what they will not experience is that sense of intimate participation in either a relationship or a situation outside their scripted roles. Both women will be, and are, loving and concerned mothers (and Dolly's sense of identity with her children is most vividly described) and both women have known times of happiness with their husbands. It is not that either Kitty or Dolly lack continuing and satisfactory relationships with their children and their kin. The absence in their existence – and the difference between their situation and that of Anna – is that neither will ever know, however fleetingly, the liberating possibility of becoming something other than what they are. Staying within the limits of conventional behaviour is what guarantees the health and happiness of Kitty and the continued existence of Dolly, but moving outside the limits of convention is what allows Anna to see, however briefly, the possibility of a society and a personal existence in which men and women experience an emotional reciprocity that transcends the social limitations of their sexual roles. The strength of Kitty and Dolly is that they remain the conventional women of aristocratic Russia, and of every other known western society. Their weakness – and the psychic limitation of their situations – is that they have to remain within those social and emotional structures that guarantee social stability but are no guide, and are largely irrelevant, to individual human happiness.

The differences that Tolstoy portrays between Anna and Dolly and Kitty are, therefore, the differences between accepting and rejecting conventional models of emotional life. Anna is the heroine of the novel because she, like other nineteenth-century heroines of the novel (from Maggie Tulliver and Catherine Earnshaw to Tess and Isobel Archer), explores for the readers the limits of convention. Tolstoy, like George Eliot, the Brontës, and every other novelist of the classic European tradition, allows his heroine to ask questions about the point of obeying social rules and expectations. Other novelists allow their characters to break some rules and behave in unconventional ways, but few allow their heroines to break moral rules and escape with impunity. Even when the moral rules are arguably wrong and trivial (as in the case of Maggie Tulliver's apparent transgressions) the novelists behave with virtually unchecked moral judgement. Maggie drowns, Catherine Earnshaw dies in a loveless marriage, Gwendolen Harleth has to live out a life of moral repentence. Women novelists, just as much as Tolstoy, act towards their characters with a fierce and avenging moral sense if the character deviates from the path of true righteousness.

But what can occur in literature does not inevitably occur in life. If the wages of sin (or minor sinfulness) are endless damnation in fiction, there is little evidence to suggest that this is obviously the case in life. Tolstoy, realist and man of the world that he was, acknowledged that many married women had affairs and that many women were as preoccupied as Anna with their appearance and the pursuit of what Tolstoy (in his morality of both the real and the fictional world) judged as essentially trivial. We know from biographical evidence that Tolstoy loathed his wife's interest in dress and in matters of personal vanity, and was vehement in his condemnation of those preoccupations which he defined as frivolous or vain. What he respected most about women was their performance as mothers. Frightful scenes occurred between Tolstoy and his wife when it became apparent that she could not breast-feed their second child, and throughout the Tolstoys' stormy marriage – and the birth of their thirteen children – husband and wife endured sharp and harsh daily encounters over every detail of the management of the children and the household. What seems to emerge from accounts of the Tolstoys' relationship is a constant battle between Tolstoy's sense of moral right and the ability of others, most crucially Sonya, to implement his understanding of the world. Tolstoy was apparently convinced of his perfect rational understanding and judgement of the world. Unfortunately difficulties arose about the willingness of others to agree with this understanding. Up to and including the very moment of his death, Tolstoy was convinced that Sonya did nothing except thwart his will and, most fundamentally, his understanding.

It is apparent from Tolstoy's diary that he was convinced of his own good judgement. Towards the end of 1899 (and eleven years before his death) he wrote on the subject of marriage:

> The chief cause of unhappiness in married life is that people have been taught to think that marriage means happiness. The incentive for marriage is sex attraction, which takes the form of promises and hopes of happiness – a view supported by public opinion and by literature. But marriage cannot cause happiness. Instead, it always means torture, with which man has to pay for satisfying his sex urge. These tortures are lack of freedom, servility, safety, revulsion, all sorts of moral and physical defects in one's mate, which one is forced to endure, such as temper, stupidity, dishonesty, vanity, drunkenness, laziness, greed, cupidity and immorality – all defects that it is much more difficult to endure in others than in oneself and which make one suffer as if they were one's own – and such physical imperfections as ugliness, slovenliness, odours, diseases, insanity and many others that are even more unbearable ... the more happiness people expect of marriage, the more they suffer.... Escape from torture is not in expecting happiness, but in anticipating the worst, and being prepared to bear it. If a man expects everything mentioned in the opening of *A Thousand and One Nights*, if a man expects drunkenness, stench, and revolting diseases, then he may overlook such minor defects as stubbornness, duplicity, and even drunkenness, cease suffering, and be happy in the realisation that worse possible things – insanity, cancer, and whatever else is mentioned in *A Thousand and One Nights* – are absent. Such a state of mind will make a man really appreciate everything good.[1]

This passage is remarkable in the depiction of Tolstoy's perception of the possible ills and shortcomings of a wife – a perception that bears little resemblance to the Sonya Tolstoy who shines in many accounts of Tolstoy's life as a model example of a faithful, bourgeois wife.

Unfortunately, the one person who did not see Sonya Tolstoy as a model wife was her husband. Indeed, the very last act of

Tolstoy's life was, quite literally, a flight from his wife. Just over a week before he died, Tolstoy ran away from Sonya, and home, leaving behind a note in which he said:

> My departure will be bitter news for you and I am sorry, but please understand and believe when I say that I could not have done anything else. My position in the house has become unbearable. In addition to everything else, I can no longer live in the luxurious surroundings in which I have been living, and I am doing what old men of my age should do: I am leaving mundane affairs so I can spend the remaining days of my life in peace and solitude. If you learn where I am, please understand and do not come after me. Your arrival would only make our situation more difficult without altering my decision. I am grateful to you for the forty eight years of honest life you have spent with me, and I ask you to forgive me for everything I have done to you, just as I am forgiving you from the bottom of my heart for anything you might have done to me. I hope you will accept the new position in which my departure places you and you will not harbour any ill-will for me. If you wish to communicate with me, speak to Alexandra. She will know where I am and will forward anything important. She cannot tell where I am because I have her promise not to reveal my whereabouts to anyone.[2]

The flight from Sonya and home did not serve Tolstoy well; ten days later he was dead. Cutting the ties that bind had cost Tolstoy his life, and although to die at the age of 82 was scarcely premature it was perhaps the case that the support Tolstoy received from Sonya – however unsatisfactory in his view – was fundamental to his existence.

This biographical instance – and the reference to the fraught and often unhappy marriage of the Tolstoys – is introduced here to emphasize a point that Tolstoy attempted to make in his novels as much as in his own life: namely, that human beings are imprisoned in their desires and needs – and both these emotions frequently contrast and contradict the rational understanding and will of individuals. From evidence of the domestic life of the Tolstoys it is apparent that the couple fought and disagreed throughout their marriage and that time did not diminish the extent to which they could irritate and enrage each other. Profound social and political disagreements fuelled emotional differences and the antagonisms that developed late in their marriage were as charged and as passionate as any that had existed earlier. Time did not mellow the feelings of the Tolstoys for each other. So the author of *Anna Karenina* never, in fact, found that relative peacefulness that he allows Levin and Kitty or Natasha and Pierre. Whatever the limitations of these households, and these marriages, Tolstoy's accounts of them suggest a mutual accommodation and acceptance of the limitations of the other party. Here we might surmise that what Tolstoy does in *Anna Karenina* and *War and Peace* he could not do in real life – separate sexual appeal and domestic harmony. Anna represents sexuality, and remains removed from the household and its essential concerns, whilst Kitty and Natasha (both women married to men considerably older than themselves and already possessing a considerable sexual and emotional history) immerse themselves in domestic life and rapidly turn their backs on sexual display.

In *Anna Karenina* we have, arguably, a novel that separates in the most conventional and mundane way seductive women from good domestic partners. In real life we know that Tolstoy was constantly tormented by his desire for his wife and what infuriated him was both this desire and his wife's refusal to surrender her judgement and her understanding to his. On frequent occasions Sonya Tolstoy simply took no notice of her husband and made autonomous decisions about the conduct of the household or the care of the children which either did not meet with Tolstoy's approval or stem from his evaluation of a particular situation. Sonya, to Tolstoy's evident fury, often acted like a mature, adult human being with rights to make decisions and act as an effective social being. Such a stance was frequently deeply infuriating to Tolstoy, who expected from his wife both complete acquiescence in all matters to do with relations with the personal and social world and absolute calm and toleration in dealing with the multitude of domestic concerns that inevitably beset a large family. Tolstoy had hoped to find the partner who would provide him with escape from illicit sexual passion, loneliness and the rootlessness of a bachelor existence. What he found, inevitably, was a human being with her own needs and difficulties who was incapable of fulfilling the many, and contradictory, roles that Tolstoy, children, and family life imposed on her.

So what Tolstoy did in *Anna Karenina* was, in effect, to separate different strands of need and identify them with particular women. Tolstoy's needs were, in a sense, essentially modern ones, in that he expected his wife to fulfil all those needs – domestic, personal and sexual – that have now come to be imposed on, and expected of, twentieth-century western women. Although *Anna Karenina* is a novel deeply rooted in nineteenth-century pre-revolutionary Russia and in the nineteenth-century narrative tradition of the novel, it is also entirely contemporary in the emotional aspirations which the male characters hope for in their wives and sexual partners. *Anna Karenina* can be read as the tragedy of an individual woman, but also as a precursor of the common disappointments of twentieth-century marriage, marriage that is associated with romance and individualized sexual desire. Anna may be a metaphor for female sexuality, but she may also be a symbol of all those disappointments which thousands of people in the west experience in the very relationship which is supposed to provide the most intimate of human satisfactions.

The major female characters of *Anna Karenina* – Kitty, Dolly, and Anna herself – are all identified with particular forms of marriage and sets of expectations. The two cases of greatest marital or personal disappointment are clearly those of Anna and Vronsky and Oblonsky and Dolly. But both these relationships, at least on the part of the women, begin from the same starting point: the female characters feel particularly 'in love' with the man, and organize their feelings around that sentiment known as romance. Where the two relationships differ is in the attitude of the two women to how their relationships should be consummated and contained. For Dolly, it is apparent that 'love and marriage go together like a horse and a carriage', whilst for Anna the notion of marriage to Vronsky is deeply problematic. Thus the men involved stand in quite different relationships to the women: for Oblonsky it is apparent that marriage is a necessary evil. Conditioned to expect that 'ordinary' men get married, Oblonsky gets himself married, but his commitment to the state is never more than partial and he is happier spending his time either with men or with the women with whom he has illicit sexual encounters. Oblonsky needs a wife because conventional bourgeois men need households, and households need wives to run and manage them. The expectations of Oblonsky and Dolly to marriage therefore begin as dissimilar. Dolly has high hopes of a rewarding, faithful, and supportive relationship with her husband and in those hopes is ultimately disappointed. Anna's worldliness does not allow her to suppose that marriage is the romantic relationship that Dolly sees (or saw) it as; her resistance to marriage is accentuated by the enthusiasm of Vronsky to embrace bourgeois respectability and to abandon the endless ambiguities and difficulties of a non-married and unconventional relationship.

When Kitty and Levin marry, Tolstoy tells us that the men talk throughout the ceremony, whilst 'the women were absorbed in watching every detail of the service, which is so close to their hearts'. Dolly, in particular, is deeply affected by the marriage ceremony:

> Her eyes were wet and she could not have spoken without bursting into tears. She rejoiced for Kitty and Levin, and her thoughts went back to her own wedding. Her glance kept straying to the beaming Oblonsky and, forgetting the present, she remembered only her young and innocent love. She recalled not herself only, but all her woman-friends and acquaintances; thought of them on the one day of their triumph when, like Kitty, they had stood beneath the nuptial crown, with love, hope, and dread in their hearts, renouncing the past and stepping forward into the mysterious future ... the women spectators, who were quite strangers, looked on breathless with excitement, afraid of missing a single movement or expression of the bride or bridegroom. Annoyed with the men for their indifference, they did not answer and often did not hear their joking or irrelevant observations.[3]

The ceremony is deeply resonant for Dolly, for, as Tolstoy

suggests, she has lost few of her innocent hopes about the unity of love and marriage. Oblonsky, it is also apparent from the ceremony, has no more romantic thoughts about marriage than he ever had; his attitude to Levin throughout the period of Levin's betrothal and marriage is that of avuncular joviality. He regards Levin's high hopes of marriage as naïve, and is amused rather than impressed by Levin's idealistic expectations of his forthcoming marriage. Worldly libertine that he is, Oblonsky regards Levin with the fond detachment of an older, more cynical, brother.

Just as the marriage of Levin and Kitty is Tolstoy's idealization of marriage so it represents for other characters the touchstone for their own relationships. And this dimension of the marriage is accompanied by another function – that it serves to emphasize Tolstoy's assertion in *Anna Karenina* that there are a set of experiences that are common for all men and all women in marriage. Tolstoy is not arguing for a man's view of marriage – any more than he is arguing for a woman's view of marriage. On the other hand he is suggesting that it is virtually inevitable that women will become preoccupied with domestic concerns and that men will find these preoccupations tedious and trivial. But what Tolstoy questions are the different perceptions and aspirations that different men and women bring to the realities of the domestic sexual division of labour. Dolly and Kitty welcome domestic concerns and regard them as a natural and inevitable part of marriage. Anna regards them with an indifference close to distaste. Levin and Vronsky, however widely separated in moral terms, are deeply interested in their households and their estates. Oblonsky matches his sister's distance from domestic concerns. Brother and sister are separated from the other characters by their relative indifference to the conditions and details of family life.

Yet at the same time as Oblonsky and Anna are united in their attitude to domestic life, they are disunited – and at opposite ends of a continuum – in their attitude to the nature of marriage and the proper relationship of the sexes. Oblonsky's attitude is that of conventional bourgeois man: wives are to be respected, if not necessarily honoured, and marriage cannot be expected to fulfil all human needs. As suggested earlier, Oblonsky cannot see anything particularly wrong in his liaison with the governess (or subsequently the dancer). But Anna, the bourgeois woman who abandons the domestic hearth, does not accept the convenient distinctions of bourgeois life. She is not prepared to remain Vronsky's mistress and live with Karenin, nor is she prepared to become the respectable wife.

What begins to emerge from looking at the characters in *Anna Karenina* in relationship to each other – rather than as isolated individuals – is that their perception of each other affects their own behaviour and their understanding of their own particular situation. Dolly becomes more reconciled to her own unhappy marriage after seeing Anna and Vronsky 'at home'; Anna finds the sight of the domestic bliss of Kitty and Levin unenviable, whilst Kitty's perception of Anna's situation only serves to increase her own happiness and contentment. Therein lies part of the nature of happiness – that it is constructed through reflections upon the lives of others. In this sense, Anna's unhappiness is as necessary to the contentment of Kitty and the minimal satisfaction of Dolly as Dolly's misery is confirming to Anna's own sense of the viability and centrality of Vronsky's love for her.

The women in *Anna Karenina* thus provide for each other important guidelines to their own behaviour, particularly in the negative sense of what they wish to avoid in human relations. The male characters have much the same function for each other. Oblonsky and Vronsky are the people that Levin does not want to be, just as his connubial isolation and domesticity have no attraction for Oblonsky or Vronsky. But from the point of view of a contemporary reading of *Anna Karenina*, and certainly from a point of view which is informed by feminism, two questions about Anna remain. The first is whether the fates of the female characters are in any sense 'realistic', or merely a male literary fantasy about what happens to unconventional women; second, there is the issue of whether Tolstoy offers anything approaching an analysis of the situation of women, rather than a moral tract (however brilliant in literary terms) about how to conduct sexual relationships. If

Anna Karenina emerges as a didactic novel, informed chiefly by patriarchal values, then Anna is, in a paradoxical sense, a heroine, since what she does is struggle against the boundaries and constraints of conventional bourgeois morality. If, on the other hand, *Anna Karenina* is more than a tract about how to behave in late nineteenth-century Russia, then Anna is an anti-heroine, in that far from escaping from conventional perceptions of sexuality and morality, Anna is deeply bound by these conventions and hostile to the development of a female selfhood which is not dependent on male admiration and desire.

From what Tolstoy tells us about Anna, we know that she is concerned about her appearance, her sexual powers, and her place in society. At one time or another she may deny all these concerns but nevertheless she consistently maintains an interest in dress, in Vronsky's feeling for her, and a deep sensitivity to the behaviour of others towards her. Of these elements one is perhaps especially significant: Anna's perception and projection of emotional need. What obsesses her increasingly as the novel moves towards its tragic end is whether or not she can continue to arouse Vronsky's desire. When she feels that she cannot, and suspects (however mistakenly) that his sexual ardour is failing, then she becomes deeply distressed, depressed, and aggressive. Of all these states, it is the aggression that is most indicative of the frustrations of Anna's situation: that women in conventional society are not supposed to possess or to demonstrate an independent sexuality, and certainly not a capacity for sexual desire that can express itself freely. Vronsky is 'allowed' to desire Anna, Anna is not 'allowed' to desire Vronsky. The fact that Vronsky's desire for Anna is only constructed out of Anna's provocative personal vanity, makes her all the more frustrated by the conventions that she is trapped by.

It is difficult to see Anna as anything other than a woman created entirely by patriarchal sexuality, which denies women access to their own sexuality by refusing the social and emotional means to negotiate sexual equality. Yet for all this, and despite considerable evidence to suggest that Anna is merely a 'bad woman' whom Tolstoy sets out to punish (she is, in effect, the very expression of all that Tolstoy found so threatening and frightening about female sexuality and, indeed, women in general), there is another possible interpretation of Anna: that although conventional in the sense in which she constructs sexual desire, she is unconventional enough, and critical enough of the status quo, to make *Anna Karenina* a novel that is subversive of the patriarchal order rather than just another example (if the definitive example) of the western patriarchal novel.

The striking feature of Tolstoy's own attitude to Anna is an attraction which is as strong as his accompanying repulsion. In describing Anna, he does so with love and sympathy. Although he acknowledges from the beginning Anna's shortcomings he is also, quite as much as Vronsky, attracted to Anna, and disinterested in Kitty and Dolly once Anna has appeared. Yet, despite his attraction and fascination, Tolstoy, as much as Vronsky, cannot adequately place or locate her. Anna rises out of Tolstoy's imagination and his literary genius, but once conceived, this figure of immense seductive power and tremendous vitality becomes intensely problematic. What is to be done with her? And what is to be done with those individuals, particularly if they happen to be women, who suggest that the constraints of the conventional world are neither necessary nor final? Tolstoy's solution is, of course, to produce a character who is fatally flawed by unreasonable passion. In this way, he can suggest that such strength that Anna might have possessed is the result of desperate need rather than real emotional integrity. Anna thus becomes a figure who can be rejected as an ideal, and as a possible example to others.

The three central female characters in *Anna Karenina* represent those three aspects of the patriarchal imagination which have commonly been identified as the limitations of patriarchal fantasies of women. Anna represents the potent sexuality of women, Dolly the domesticated and endlessly loyal wife, and Kitty the child-bride whom it is the responsibility of men to educate into the ways of the sexual and the social world. All three characters are expected by Tolstoy to stay properly placed and accept their enduring fate. Attempts by these women to negotiate alternatives for themselves are scorned by the author. Anna is not 'allowed' to become respectable; sexuality and sexual passion – particularly if openly expressed – have to remain outside society. Equally respectable women do not meet Levin's brother's mistress, so respectable women do not meet Anna, indeed, they turn their backs on her. What is more significant, women become deeply suspicious of the attractions of Anna. For example, when Levin meets Anna after her separation from Karenin, Kitty becomes fiercely jealous; when Levin returns home after the meeting, Kitty confronts him with the accusation that:

> 'You have fallen in love with that hateful woman! She has bewitched you! I saw it in your eyes. Yes, yes! What will be the end of it? You were drinking and drinking at the club, and gambling, and then you went ... to her, of all people! No, we must go away.... I shall go away tomorrow.'
>
> It was long before Levin could pacify his wife. At last he succeeded in calming her only by acknowledging that the wine he had drunk, together with his sense of pity, had been too much for him and he had succumbed to Anna's artful spell; and by promising that in future he would avoid her. He was sincerest of all when he confessed that living for so long in Moscow with nothing to do but eat, drink, and gossip was beginning to demoralise him. They talked till three o'clock in the morning. Only by three o'clock were they sufficiently reconciled to be able to go to sleep.[4]

The passage contains many of the ingredients of those commonly observed patterns of western sexual relations: that men frequently lie to women about their sexual and emotional feelings, that women are deeply jealous of other women (and especially of other women with whom men have some form of prior relationship) and that sexual attraction is perceived as witchcraft. When Levin agrees to Kitty's jealous accusations he does so because the habits and the expectations of that society have left him little alternative. If he were to admit to Kitty that he found Anna attractive as a woman, it would be tantamount to admitting that although he had chosen Kitty as his wife, and made what is supposed to be a commitment to fidelity, he still has the capacity to recognize sexual appeal, and respond to it. What Kitty in effect forces Levin to do is to make Anna into the archetypal 'other woman' of western romance and fiction – the woman who lives by sexual appeal and whose central concern is to attract other women's husbands. So Kitty – not Levin – bans Anna's entry into the social circle of the Levins. It is jealousy between women about women's relationships with men that separates women and makes them the fierce defenders of their own sexual space and their husband's or lover's attentions.

So Kitty the child-bride is also the passionate defender of her home and her husband's thoughts. But this almost violent defence of her private space is more than matched by that of Levin. When their guest Vasenka appears to become over friendly with Kitty, and addresses her in a way that Levin regards as dangerously close to intimacy, he insists on Vasenka leaving their home. To the amazement of Oblonsky and Kitty's mother, Levin almost literally throws Vasenka out of the house. Domestic space, the private space of marriage, is not to be violated, even by the mere suggestion that husbands, and wives, might still exist as sexual beings. Although marriage makes heterosexual activity legitimate, it does so only within the narrow limits of sexual relations between man and wife. The constraints of this situation are rapidly realized by Kitty and Levin; she becomes jealous of Levin's conversation with Anna, he becomes jealous of his wife's conversation with Vasenka.

But both Kitty and Levin accept these constraints and with them an entirely modern, and bourgeois, concept of marriage. Levin makes it clear to Kitty before their marriage that he has had numerous sexual relationships but that once married he will renounce such behaviour. For him, marriage is a relationship with one woman, a woman in whom he invests all his hopes and expectations. Part of the appeal of Kitty is that she is so different from the other women he has known. In all Levin's romantic musings about Kitty, one feature of his beloved occurs over and over again – her innocence. To Levin, quite as much as to Kitty's father, the quality of the young, modest, virgin is a quality almost worthy of beatification.

When, for example, Kitty is examined (prior to her marriage) by a male doctor, it is Kitty's father who is the most affronted by the ritual, and who is the only member of the household – other than Kitty – who recognizes that Kitty's malady is less a physical illness than a broken heart over the defection of Vronsky from a pursuit of Kitty to a pursuit of Anna. Talking to Dolly of her predicament, Kitty explains that she now thinks nothing except 'vile' thoughts:

> 'I have nothing to make me miserable,' she said when she had grown calmer, 'but can you understand that everything seems vile, odious, coarse to me, myself most of all? You cannot imagine what vile thoughts I have about everything.'[5]

If we substitute sexual desire for 'vile thoughts', then some of Kitty's misery becomes clear. Expected to play the part of the young, innocent girl, and to allow Vronsky to pursue her, Kitty observes, to her immense chagrin, the enticement of Vronsky by Anna's explicit display of sexual power and appeal. Anna's behaviour, Kitty recognizes, is how she might have behaved had she not been bound by the expectations of the innocent girl. Even more, what Kitty perhaps recognizes is that she has the capacity to act as Anna did. Indeed, Kitty acknowledges, if only to herself, the limits of that innocence which is so alluring to both Levin and her father. So in Kitty and Anna we have the two faces of women: on one side innocence, on the other sexual power. To women, this duality is nothing amazing or surprising. Kitty's mother is not inclined to view her daughter as the same innocent that her father perceives. Dolly is well aware that her own daughters possess the ability to behave innocently in order to secure their desires. Amongst these women there is the unstated knowledge of the kind of behaviour expected of them, and a perception of the pressures that produce the distortions of meaning and motive that are tacitly understood.

As a tract on how to conduct sexual relations, the moral of *Anna Karenina* might be that honesty does not always secure happiness. When Oblonsky is honest with his wife about his mistress, it causes endless unhappiness. Anna's honesty with

Karenin results in separation. Levin's honesty with Kitty about his past produces jealousy. The impulse to confess, to tell intimates 'everything', involves many of the central characters in difficulties and tortuous explanations and justifications. The problem for all these characters is that they cannot be wholly open and honest; what is not communicated or confessed are their real feelings and desires. For example, Oblonsky confesses to his wife that he has had an affair; he only admits to himself (and to the readers) his attitude to the affair. Even then, although he tells us that he needs sexual relationships outside his marriage, he cannot reveal why this might be the case. So Oblonsky, like Anna and Levin, goes half way down the road to revelation, but in doing so produces a good deal more deception.

Of all the characters in the novel it is Levin and Anna who most grapple with the issue of maintaining what they see as honesty in their personal relationships. Both characters put great store on sincerity, and an openness of feeling. Vronsky is attractive to Anna partly because he seems to have none of the emotional distance and evasiveness that ultimately so repels her about Karenin. Levin finds Kitty appealing because he is convinced of her total inability to deceive. Man and woman, they look for a perfect, undistorted, reflection of their own selves in the other person. Thus Levin, who wishes above all to be good, in some absolute sense, values the apparent confirmation of himself that he can find in Kitty. Anna, who wishes above all else to be sexually desired and sexually essential, appeals to Vronsky (and is attracted to Vronsky) for the apparently endless desire that he can evoke. When Levin sees other couples dissembling, he is shocked and irritated. Observing Oblonsky greeting Dolly, Levin

> ... who a minute before had been in the happiest frame of mind, now looked darkly at everyone, feeling out of temper with everything.
>
> 'Who was it he kissed yesterday with those lips?' he thought, looking at Oblonsky's tender demonstrations to his wife. He glanced at Dolly, and did not like her either.
>
> 'She doesn't believe in his love. So what is she pleased about?

Revolting!' thought Levin . . .

Even his brother, Koznyshev, who had also come out on to the steps, irritated him with the show of cordiality with which he greeted Oblonsky, for whom, as Levin knew, he had neither liking nor esteem.

And Vasenka, too, was hateful as she shook hands with the fellow, with her air of being too holy for words, when all she thought about was getting married.

And most hateful of all was Kitty for falling in with the cheerful satisfaction of this gentleman who appeared to consider his visit in the country a piece of good fortune for himself and all concerned; and particularly objectionable was that special smile of hers with which she responded to his smiles.[6]

During this visit – of Kitty's relations, and their acquaintance Vasenka – Levin confronts what is, for him, a deeply disturbing possibility: that the child-bride whose innocence he so valued is also a woman who can recognize and evoke sexual desire and admiration in other men. In hoping for a wife who would force him from illicit sexual relations Levin places Kitty on that traditional pedestal of captured and imprisoned wives – the pedestal of admiration that puts women above sexual pleasure and denies their own personal inclinations and desires. Levin cannot entertain the idea that Kitty is a sexual being – a wife certainly, and a mother certainly, but not a sexual being, and least of all one with the capacity for individual choice. The problem, perhaps, is less that Levin fears that Kitty will become involved in some real liaison (however brief and superficial) than that her behaviour will provoke in him all those patterns of behaviour that he had expected his marriage to eliminate. The promise of Kitty, and the absurd bashfulness and timidity of Levin's initial relations with her, lay, therefore, in the hope that virginity and innocence could vanquish the unruly passions that Levin found so shameful. Kitty is therefore left in the situation of minimal possible participation in social life, and her own development as a person is doomed to the perpetually retarded existence of a domestically confined and innocent girl. Just before the novel closes we see Levin furious at his wife for taking a walk with their baby son. Part of Levin's anger is admittedly due to anxiety for the safety of his wife and

his son, but the short incident (in which Kitty smiles 'timidly' at
Levin and Levin rebukes Kitty as if she were a naughty child)
suggests that ideally Kitty should have sought permission for
her promenade. Obviously Levin, like any fond husband and
father, does not want danger to befall his wife and son, but the
incident evokes the suspicion that Levin does not really think
that Kitty can make adult decisions and look after herself.

This aspect of Levin's perception of Kitty is to be seen more
clearly in the visit of Levin and Kitty to Levin's dying brother.
Levin at first refuses Kitty's request to be allowed to accompany
him. Levin states quite categorically that '... that women is
there, with whom you can't associate.'[7] Purity such as Kitty's is
not to be sullied by contact with women such as Maria
Nikolayevna, and youth and innocence are not to be contaminated by experiences of worlds other than those of utterly conventional morality. Although eventually Kitty persuades Levin
to take her with him, we are told that: 'The mere idea of his
wife, his Kitty, in the same room with a common wench set him
shuddering with repulsion and horror.'[8]

The visit begins as badly as Levin had feared, with Kitty and
Maria Nikolayevna blushing at the sight of each other and
covered in mutual unease and discomfort. Eventually, however,
a *modus vivendi* is achieved, largely through the common
female condition of domestic labour. Kitty moves into the
filthy, sloppy hotel and cleans up, in doing so enlisting Maria's
help. Together the women sweep and dust, so that the
embarrassing problems of a meeting between a fallen woman
and a respectable wife disappear in the mists of Kitty's aromatic
vinegar. Levin has to admit that: ' "Yes, you see, that woman,
Maria Nikolayevna, did not know how to manage all this," said
Levin. "And ... I must own I'm very very glad you came. You
are purity itself ..." '[9]

So the good woman is also the useful woman, and good, pure
women are able to manage social situations because they do not
present to the world an ambiguous face. The waiter who would
have done nothing for Maria obeys Kitty's commands and
although the waiter probably had fewer doubts about Kitty's
ability to pay him, we are also led to believe that something of

the 'quiet persistence' of Kitty impresses him as well. Thus what emerges in Kitty is an equation: purity equals goodness equals effectiveness. Because Kitty is absolutely good – at least as far as Levin is concerned – so her actions are not diverted by 'impure' or confusing motives. The 'message' that comes across from Kitty is that of a wholly useful person, who will do the right thing and who will act with the perfect sureness of absolute moral integrity. The only shortcoming that Kitty might have – and hence Levin's constant watchfulness – is a slight tendency to provoke the attractions of other men. More cynical observers of Kitty might say that what Levin cannot see in Kitty, and indeed in other women as well, is the endless possibility of those sisters under the skin, Mrs O'Grady and the Colonel's Lady. Levin loves Kitty because she is so apparently distant from sexual desire. But it is evident from Kitty's initial attraction to Vronsky that she is no innocent to the realms of passion. She, just as much as Levin, has to repress that possibility in order to maintain the moral foundation of her marriage. Kitty therefore abjures Anna just as Levin condemns Vasenka. Indeed, it is essential to Kitty's position within the marriage that she does deny Anna, for the demon sexuality must be kept out of the safe haven of the home. Once allowed in, the household is threatened by those awful conflicts and jealousies that have so disturbed the Karenins and the Oblonskys and denied domestic bliss to Anna and Vronsky.

The problematic woman in *Anna Karenina* might be, therefore, not Kitty or Anna, since they represent two sides of a highly conventional coin, but Dolly. Kitty is the woman innocent of sexuality, Anna the woman inspired and motivated by it. As such, they are both conventional figures – the good woman and the fallen temptress. Dolly, however, is a more ambivalent case. As inspired by romance as Kitty or Anna, as initially innocent in appearance as Kitty, and as disappointed in marriage as Anna, she stands at the centre of a continuum which has at its extremes sexual experience and passionate need and at the other sexual innocence and passivity. But what Dolly represents, unlike Anna and Kitty, is reality. In terms of the actual situation of women in nineteenth-century Russia (or anywhere in nineteenth-century Europe or North America) Dolly corresponds far more to what we know actually existed. No doubt there were Kittys and Annas, the child-brides adored by their husbands and the stunningly seductive women radiating sexual power, but these figures were probably more often fantasy than fact, and even more often moulded by experience and circumstance into women like Dolly. We see Kitty as a young bride with one child, but it is quite likely that in a few years she will also become the tired mother of what Queen Victoria used to call '*une nombreuse famille*'. Equally, we see Anna as a radiant beauty but we know that she is terrified of becoming old and tired – her deliberate rejection of maternity and endless pregnancies shocks Dolly by its clear-eyed recognition of the fragility of sexual attraction.

So Dolly is at once an ordinary woman – in that her circumstances correspond to those of millions of other women – and a woman who evokes strong feelings in others in that she represents for both Anna and Kitty what they do not wish for themselves. Indeed, Dolly is arguably the measure by which Kitty and Anna assess and plan their lives. Furthermore, what is interesting about their assessment of Dolly's life is that both Anna and Kitty – in other ways radically separated by both inclination and personal situation – come to the same conclusions about how unenviable is Dolly's lot in life. Anna, after all, has to be summoned from home to sort out the domestic fracas at the Oblonskys' and her assessment of Dolly's situation is such as to make her own life instantly attractive. Marriage to the unfaithful, unattentive and shiftless Oblonsky is hardly an appealing prospect, but it is Kitty, and not Anna, who points out the limitations of the marriage with particular clarity, and a certain cruelty. Whilst Anna persuades Dolly to agree to a reconciliation with Oblonsky, Kitty, on a subsequent occasion, taunts Dolly by referring to Oblonsky's failings. When Dolly tries to console Kitty at the defection of Vronsky Kitty lashes out at her sister:

'I can't understand what you want to torment me for I've told you, and I say it again, that I have some pride and never, *never* would I do what you do – go back to a man who has betrayed you, who loves another woman. I can't understand you, I can't understand you! You may do it, but I cannot.'[10]

Dolly is both hurt and wounded by Kitty's attack, even though there is no lasting estrangement between the sisters and their relationship remains a close and sympathetic one. But what Kitty reveals in this moment of temper is her own fear of a marriage like that of Dolly. For both Anna and Kitty the difficulties and humiliations that Dolly faces are touchstones by which they measure their own aspirations and pride. Both, having seen the miseries inflicted on women by unfaithful husbands, want a husband, a lover, who is sexually and emotionally faithful and exclusive, and both, seeing the material difficulties that Dolly is always confronted by, want a husband who is effective as a provider. Just as Anna is to patch up the Oblonsky marriage in emotional terms (although not entirely successfully) so Levin is later to provide help and support to maintain Dolly's household.

When Dolly goes to stay at Vronsky's country estate (and in doing so shows generous broadmindedness in overlooking the unconventional relationship of Anna and Vronsky) she takes with her a much patched and darned bed-jacket. Arriving at Vronsky's beautifully kept house and confronted with the elegance of the domestic arrangements, Dolly is suddenly much ashamed of this garment:

> She was ashamed to let her see the patched dressing-jacket, which, as ill-luck would have it, had been packed for her by mistake. The very patches and darns of which she had been so proud at home now made her feel uncomfortable.[11]

Yet by the end of the visit Dolly has become not merely less intimidated by all the wealth and opulence of Vronsky's household but positively uncomfortable in its midst. She cannot wait to return to her own home and children. Although sympathetic to Anna and Vronsky, she has not established any real rapport with them (Vronsky's view of Dolly is that she is '*excessivement terre-à-terre*') and feels an unbridgeable gap between her world and theirs. The difference, however, is that although Dolly can settle back into her world, and is confirmed in her own life by a visit to Anna's, Anna herself is disturbed by Dolly. Anna confirms Dolly, but Dolly˙unsettles Anna and makes apparent, once again, the separation that Anna must accept from conventional society.

So the beautiful Anna, the handsome Vronsky, and their apparently great and all-encompassing love are, if not brought to nothing by comparison with Dolly, then at least revealed as resting on insubstantial foundations. Wealth sustains Vronsky's household in a way that Dolly has never known. Nevertheless Dolly's patched bed-jacket suggests a capacity to maintain and sustain a social and material world that is absent in Anna. By comparison with Dolly (who knows everything about the management of her household down to the last rouble) Anna knows nothing of the domestic management of her household. As Dolly notices, Anna is at a loss to locate her daughter's toys and is a stranger to the nursery. All this is alien to Dolly, who has nursed her own children through childhood illnesses and performed much of the domestic labour of her home herself. Dolly can clearly create a domestic world, in the most basic and mundane sense of organizing a regular supply of food and clean clothes. What Vronsky so cavalierly dismisses as Dolly's excessive down-to-earthness is the very quality that Anna lacks and which eventually jeopardizes the relationship of Anna and Vronsky.

Ideals of womanhood, of masculinity, of love, and of conjugal relations are all, in one way or another, reduced to ashes in *Anna Karenina*. Levin has to learn that the idealized Kitty is also the stubborn wife pre-occupied with domestic trifles. Anna has to endure (but cannot accept) the weakening bonds of sexual desire, and Vronsky and Karenin, in their unhappy relationships with Anna, react with a similar inflexibility to the realization that the enticing object of their love is riddled with insecurities and unmet needs. Dolly and Oblonsky, as ineffective as they are in their different ways, proceed along a commonplace path that is unmarked by beliefs in absolute principles and unarguable truths. Levin and Anna have to acknowledge the disparity between experience and projected ideals. But for all that, Levin is a man, and as such he can find ways of accommodating himself to the tarnished nature of human and social reality. Anna is a woman, and for her, coming to terms with reality would involve attachment to domestic life and a patriarchal marriage. At least for Anna, Dolly represents a particularly unhappy but utterly common-place example of this life, and thus it is not entirely surprising that she clings to her own – ultimately tragic – vision of what she wants from life. Dolly, the representative *par excellence* of the ordinary condition of woman, demonstrates all too clearly the price of obedience to patriarchal notions of marriage, sexuality, and domestic compliance. The cruel paradox, which Anna cannot but perceive, is that in the acceptance of her lot lies Dolly's strength. By coming to terms with Oblonsky's unfaithfulness and fickleness, Dolly becomes her own woman in a way that Anna, clinging to the hope of Vronsky's love, never achieves. If there is a real heroine in *Anna Karenina* then that honour might well go to Dolly, rather than Anna herself.

Chapter Four

WHAT IS A GOOD WOMAN?

W HEN TOLSTOY wrote *Anna Karenina* he was attempting to move towards a state of moral and emotional equilibrium in his own life. Establishing a viable morality was a central part of this process, as he was coming to terms with his own past (particularly his sexual past) and working out some kind of *modus vivendi* with his wife. *Anna Karenina* is thus a deeply autobiographical and subjective work in which Tolstoy explores those problems, social and emotional, which concerned him in his own life. The fates that he assigns to his central characters are, as it were, bench-marks in a continuing attempt to resolve this question and the ethical problems it poses. Very broadly, he is suggesting that women should locate their influence and activity in the home and that men should engage in useful and productive work without compromising their relations with others in the private domain. However, this simple philosophy leaves many questions and problems unanswered, problems arising from differences in power, influence, and resources and the consequences of living by a morality that is anchored firmly in the satisfaction of individual interests.

What confronts us, particularly in the figure of Anna, is the question of how women should live, and the kinds of priorities that they should value. Tolstoy is, at least in *War and Peace* and *Anna Karenina*, an intensely moralistic author who deals harshly with human vanities and the frailty of ideals. But whilst the central male characters – Levin, Vronsky and Karenin – do not escape unscathed, it is the women who are more harshly punished. The inequality of their respective fates tends to support the view that Tolstoy's attitude to women was one of suspicion, fear, and retribution. Anna has sinned most, so Anna must die. Dolly has 'failed' to maintain her husband's affections and so she must be punished. Kitty is young and innocent, and so she must be made aware of the realities of life by a harrowing experience while giving birth to her first child. 'In sorrow shalt thou bring forth children' thunders the Old Testament, and Tolstoy does not spare his female characters by emphasizing the painful rigours of childbirth in contrast to the enticing pleasures of sex.

It is curious that a male novelist should be so much more explicit on the subject of the rigours of childbirth and child-rearing than any of the married and unmarried female novelists of the nineteenth century. George Eliot, Jane Austen, the Brontës and Elizabeth Gaskell all allow their characters to give birth in relative privacy and comfort, whereas Tolstoy is quite explicit on the very real contemporary dangers of prolonged labour, puerperal fever, and difficulties in feeding infants. Indeed, Tolstoy is quite unambiguous on the physical suffering of motherhood, it is often painful, exhausting, and commonly fatal.

But in common with other nineteenth-century novelists, both male and female, Tolstoy does suggest the possible rewards of motherhood, and indeed of parenthood. Levin, quite as much as Kitty, is deeply attached to his son, and both Karenin and Vronsky are fiercely jealous and concerned about the children borne to them by Anna. In this respect, Tolstoy does not see motherhood as a state that separates men from women in a moral sense. It is clearly recognized in *Anna Karenina* that it is women who bear the terrors and pains of pregnancy, childbirth, and lactation. Moreover, Tolstoy fully acknowledges that even for relatively privileged women the process of becoming a mother does not cease with the birth of a child: motherhood and mothering are states that transform all women into mothers with a distinct and never-ending set of responsibilities and difficulties. But the interesting and problematic assumption of

75

Anna Karenina is that Tolstoy does not suggest that motherhood makes women into different moral beings. Mothers face the pain of physically bearing children and the endless demands of rearing them, but they do not do so as different, or transformed moral beings.

Separation of the various dimensions of motherhood – the physical process of birth, the child's dependency upon the mother and the moral obligations on women to care for and succour children – is not a separation that is commonly made either by feminist or non-feminist thinking. The Western Judeo-Christian tradition has always venerated mothers – archetypically the Virgin Mary, the mother of Jesus, who bore a child untainted by sin – and to a certain extent contemporary (and nineteenth-century) feminism has endorsed this view, albeit for different purposes. In the last decade a resurgence of feminist interest in motherhood has led to the identification of what Sara Ruddick has described as 'maternal thinking' and the distinct, and highly personalized, form of moral sensitivity suggested as characteristic of women by Carol Gilligan. In attempting to make motherhood a state whose constraints and particular demands are recognized by a society which values only very different kinds of achievement, feminists have argued that to be a mother involves the internalization and the articulation of a highly distinct form of morality. Symbolically, this form of moral concern has been expressed visually by the decoration of the barbed wire fence around Greenham Common Air Force base with the paraphernalia of infancy and childhood – nappies, toys, and babies' clothes adorn the metal fence. The point is, of course, that no mother could possibly endorse a political system that validates nuclear weapons. Motherhood is identified with, and synonymous with, caring, nurturance, and protection against life-threatening aggression be it inter-personal or inter-state.

In this analysis, and this ideology of motherhood, the mother is always the 'good' mother. As in fairy stories, good mothers care for their children and only stepmothers are associated with the more vicious and cruel behaviour of which women might be capable. But as Sara Ruddick has pointed out, maternal thinking has always been 'inauthentic'. She writes:

> By 'inauthenticity' I designate a double willingness – first, a willingness to *travailler pour l'armée* to accept the uses to which others put one's children; and second, a willingness to remain blind to the implications of those uses for the actual lives of women and children. Maternal thought embodies inauthenticity by taking on the values of the dominant culture.... As inauthenticity is lived out in maternal practice, it gives rise to values of obedience and 'being good'; that is, it is taken as an achievement to fulfill the values of the dominant culture.... Individual mothers, living out maternal thought, take on the subcultures to which they belong and with whom they are allied. Because some groups and many men are vibrantly moral, these values are not necessarily inadequate. Nevertheless, even moral groups and men almost always accept the relative subordination of women, whatever other ideals of equality and autonomy they may hold.... The strain of colluding in one's own powerlessness, coupled with the frequent and much greater strain of betraying the children one has tended, would be insupportable if conscious.[1]

This passage, written in 1982, is quoted at length because it is revealing in some of the suggestions that it makes about motherhood, suggestions that are as relevant to mothers of the 1880s as to those of the 1980s. For example, Kitty personifies the mother who, because she is married to a 'good' man herself, comes to express and live out 'good' values. Anna and Dolly, married to or living with men who are far more morally suspect or ambivalent than Levin, have to find for themselves values by which they can live, and within which they can raise their children. All three women are powerless in the civil and legal sense, yet all three have, to a greater or lesser extent, that degree of control and influence within the household that has always been exercised by women.

Dolly, Anna, and Kitty, of course, are all without any real autonomy or socially recognized power. Like women in numerous societies, they live out their lives without any significant participation in political and civil society and are people of the private world. Yet despite this common powerlessness there is also a disparity in their situations; each woman has different and distinct forms of influence and lack of control. Here what is interesting is that in each case the particular source of a character's power is also her weakness: Anna's ability to evoke a powerful sexual and emotional response is also the weakness that binds her to the fatal relationship with Vronsky; Dolly's maternal conscientiousness and concern is the quality that prevents her from taking a more assertive attitude to her husband's infidelity and incompetence, and Kitty's youth and innocence makes her vulnerable to the influence of Levin's ideas. Each woman, in her different way, has a specific form of attraction and strength which is also an Achilles' heel. Kitty personifies the woman who takes on the character of the subculture into which she marries; so – to a lesser extent – does Anna. Kitty is saved from a worse fate because Levin is honest, and, in a conventional sense, 'good', but Anna emerges from the novel as the woman who colludes in her own fate, who betrays her commitments as a mother and wife, and who is punished by Tolstoy with death.

Two conclusions emerge from this interpretation of *Anna Karenina*: the first is that, for all her failings, it is Dolly rather than Anna who is the most morally assertive character in the novel, and who thus occupies the place traditionally given to heroines. The second point is that Anna, unlike Dolly, is a deeply contradictory character, in that she takes on the characteristics of the men she is associated with, but recognizes, both consciously and unconsciously, that in doing so she betrays both herself and her children. When Sara Ruddick writes that 'the strain of colluding in one's own powerlessness, coupled with the frequent and much greater strain of betraying the children one has tended, would be insupportable if conscious' she is accurately describing Anna's situation: a woman who actively and energetically uses her sexuality within the context of unequal heterosexual relations and, in doing so, turns her back on the two children she has borne. We know from Tolstoy's account of Anna's state of mind that the loss of her son is a deep sadness and regret to her; here the insupportable actually *is* conscious and it is difficult to suppose that part of the psychic pain that Anna bears in her relationship with Vronsky is an agonizing remorse at the loss of Seriozha. The 'loss' is, in fact, a dual one; Anna loses Seriozha in the literal sense of losing day to day contact with him, but she also loses him in the sense of losing him to Karenin, to Karenin's control and to Karenin's world and values. We are told by Tolstoy that this loss is a final one. We see Seriozha growing into a young man who is already replicating his father's harsh condemnation of affectivity and sensuality and beginning to echo his father's categorization of the moral world as absolutely divided between the good and the bad. The emotional space for affection and the acceptance of physical needs as a positive part of the human condition which Anna had valued in her relationship with her son, are now all doomed to disappear.

But Anna's powerlessness (in the sense of her lack of legal control over her marital situation) and the double edged and fatally insecure nature of her sexual power make it impossible for her to do anything except live out the limitations and the contradictions of her situation. As a mother she is, to use Sara Ruddick's description, 'inauthentic', in that she is unable to assert, establish, or maintain any independent world for her children. We see her virtually ignoring her daughter by Vronsky, and we are told of the surprise of Karenin, Dolly, and even Vronsky that anyone could ignore so delightful a child. Yet we might also perceive this distant relationship between mother and child in another way – as a defence against the possible loss of another child, and the repeated agony of separation. We might also conjecture that Anna, as the mother of Vronsky's child, now living in Vronsky's house and to a large extent in Vronsky's world, has recognized that in this world the role of 'good mother' does not carry a great deal of weight. It is not expected here that mothers will live selflessly for their children, and Anna indicates in her conversation with Dolly that she appreciates that being a good mother is never going to count for a great deal with Vronsky. Certainly, he does not expect his children to be physically or socially neglected, but he does not, unlike Levin, value the concern and the care that other women might devote to their children. In his culture, parenthood expresses fertility, masculine potency, and the security of the inheritance of rank and wealth; it is not a relationship to be valued or sought for other more intangible moral and emotional reasons.

Anna, therefore, personifies the woman who is entirely at the mercy of dominant patriarchal values. It is not perhaps too much of an exaggeration to say that Anna herself virtually does not exist, except as a fictional representation of those two deeply contradictory male attitudes to women – their powerful sexuality and their complete lack of secular power and control. Quite literally, Anna has no assets in dealing with the world except the desires she can evoke in men. Only sexual desire unites her to Vronsky, and should this desire disappear – particularly on his side – then Anna is left with nothing. Even in the most personal and intimate dealings of Anna and Vronsky it is always Vronsky's sexual desire for Anna that matters: what is quite absent from *Anna Karenina*, and is one of the major silences of the novel, is any account of Anna's diminishing, or even changing, desire for Vronsky. We know that initially she is deeply drawn and attracted to Vronsky, but we are given no further indication of whether this desire is maintained, developed or even reconsidered on Anna's side. It is taken as read by a male nineteenth-century writer that what matters in sexual relationships is the desire of the man for the woman. The reverse is not considered and the belief that sexual desire works in this one-sided way is so deeply ingrained in western culture that even a feminist writer such as Simone de Beauvoir could write of male heterosexuality that it is 'commonly known that familiarity decreases desire'.

Feminists have now comprehensively documented and examined the politics of heterosexuality. This examination has pointed out the inequalities – latent and manifest – within heterosexuality, and has attacked the western assumption that male sexuality is in some absolute, trans-cultural sense always active and always seeking satisfaction in sexual relationships with women. Yet to assume this as a general belief is, of course, mistaken, since the possible and actual sexuality of women was recognized in Europe for centuries before nineteenth-century moral and religious codes inhibited its expression. What this did – and as Freud recognized – was to constitute a particular form of repression in both male and female sexuality. Tolstoy shows the human results of this repression. Anna is the victim in the case of women, but Vronsky and Karenin are also – if not equally – the victims of the suppression of femininity and affectivity in men. For those human needs Vronsky and Karenin substitute empty codes of moral conduct – a formal and bureaucratic one in Karenin's case, but in Vronsky's a code which is just as irrelevant and inadequate when it comes to confronting moral situations of some complexity and ambiguity. But what distinguishes Freud's analysis of sexual represssion from that of Tolstoy is that in Tolstoy's case, the author holds deeply felt and passionately defended moral positions about the value of sexual repression. In short, Tolstoy states his view that Anna – his metaphor for the unbridled sexual potential of women – was insufficiently civilized: she did not subordinate her passions to any recognized code, and as such she became a morally deviant person. Freud, on the other hand, might have recognized (had Anna arrived as a patient) that here was a woman whose desires were *too* inhibited and conditioned by social norms – so that her only means of expression was through a highly individualized hetero-sexuality. Anna's creativity – that urge to impose some personal mark on the world – was deeply thwarted by the strictures and circumstances, both personal and social, of her situation. So Anna is not the 'guilty' party in this analysis, nor is female sexuality the mythical evil apple which leads men astray.

But to Tolstoy, Anna is the original Eve of the nineteenth-century bourgeois male mind. Growing up in a society in which sexual relations with women were shaped by norms that separated 'good' women from sexual pleasure and personal initiative, Tolstoy worked out his morbid fantasies of female sexuality in the character of Anna. Here, dreams the author, is a bourgeois woman, a civilized and beautiful woman who is also a potent sexual being. This is no *hausfrau*, no respectable wife and mother, but a female creature for whom sexual passion is as much a part of the fabric of everyday life as food and drink. Unfortunately for Anna, and for later generations who might read *Anna Karenina* as a moral tale about the sexual transgressions of woman, Tolstoy is so much a creature of his time and his place that he cannot conceive of Anna as a triumphant and finally happy and fulfilled being. With both a sharply realistic eye (for Tolstoy did of course very accurately record the difficulties and constraints of women trying to escape from unhappy marriages in an age of the virtual impossibility of divorce and a rigorously enforced sexual moral standard) and with a deeply moralistic intent, Tolstoy condemns Anna to death and allows the risks faced by a woman in her situation to become a real and actual tragedy.

Anna is, then, moved like a puppet to her death, bringing miserable fates (as far as we know) to Seriozha, Ani, and Vronsky. The status of *Anna Karenina* as a novel remains, moreover, unchallenged as a work of genius. Indeed, *Anna Karenina* is frequently cited as the greatest novel ever written; the novel which above all others demonstrates and fulfils the promise and the craft of bourgeois critical realism. To bourgeois and socialist critics alike *Anna Karenina* is the great novel of the west. An alternative interpretation – which I wish to suggest here, together with a fuller explanation of the previous suggestion that Dolly is the real heroine of *Anna Karenina* – is that *Anna Karenina* is a deeply fatalistic work, fired and fuelled by the personal anguish and moral concern of its author. But as a dispassionate work of the portrayal of the human condition it stands at the far end of a continuum at the other end of which are novels such as those of George Eliot, Jane Austen and Thomas Mann. To a greater or lesser extent these novelists had, inevitably, their own view and interpretation of the world in which they lived – it would be impossible for any human being not to have some kind of understanding (however minimal) of their circumstances. But unlike Tolstoy these authors allow their characters the human capacity to act and to fashion their fates. With his other characters – Levin and Dolly in particular – Tolstoy demonstrates that he does recognize that human beings construct their fates. Yet in the same novel he takes as his central character not a real, creative person, but a fictionalized version of his own needs and his own projections about women. The popularity of *Anna Karenina* with male literary critics could therefore be explained as an indication of the extent to which many critics share the same fantasies about women and female sexuality as Tolstoy. In effect, *Anna Karenina* elaborates these fantasies, in that Anna presents men with the engaging fantasy of a woman who is both sexually accomplished and yet exclusive in her affections. At the same time, Anna does not become a challenge to male sexuality because in the conclusion to the novel the author makes it plain that a woman who is as committed and determined as Anna is also morally and emotionally unstable. What a consolation for bourgeois sexuality this conclusion remains: the social and moral order of properly regulated 'normal' heterosexuality remains unchallenged and Anna becomes one of those nineteenth- (and indeed twentieth-) century women whom it is possible to label as deviant or even hysterical. It was not unknown for women in nineteenth- and twentieth-century England who had borne children outside marriage to be placed in mental hospitals, and this kind of punitive institutionalization is part and parcel of the moral thinking that informs *Anna Karenina*. Tolstoy does not take Anna and Ani to a mental hospital, or an asylum, but he does make Anna commit suicide and he does condemn Ani to what in effect will be an orphan's life.

To sympathize with Anna as a heroine is difficult for a feminist reader, or perhaps for any reader with a critical awareness of some of the hidden agendas and not-so-hidden motives of fiction. Anna is certainly a victim – anyone who commits suicide after a miserable and anguished existence can hardly be seen as anything else. But to elevate Anna to the status of a heroine is more difficult, since we might expect at best some evidence that a heroine attempts to rise above her fate. It is not necessarily to judge Anna in the same way as Tolstoy, but some capacity for resistance would have to manifest itself for us to see Anna as a person of courage and valour. She is clearly capable of social recklessness (witness her appearance at the opera after her return from the country with Vronsky) but she shows little sign of reflection or an understanding of her behaviour or an attempt to come to terms with the constraints which she has, to a certain extent, imposed on herself. Without interests or occupations other than her consuming passion for Vronsky and her narcissism, she offers no model of how women might resist the strictures of conventional patriarchal authority. In fact, far from resisting conventions Anna internalizes their constraints. Anna is a poor friend to other women, and she is left in no position to challenge others' judgement of herself as a fallen woman. Her one explicit feminist statement is support for the education of women, but her behaviour in general suggests a woman who is destroyed by the patriarchal values that both separate women through their relationships with men and exaggerate the importance of men and their relationships with women. We read, admittedly, that Anna is deeply aware of the sexual double standard of nineteenth-century society but we do not see any evidence that she challenges this standard and its assumptions in her own behaviour. It is impossible not to be moved by the pathos of Anna's situation, but at the same time it is difficult to see in Anna those qualities of personal and emotional strength which we commonly associate with heroism.

On the other hand, Dolly – the rather silly, ineffectual, shabby wife who provides the first female contrast with the brilliant and beautiful Anna – is the woman who emerges from the novel as someone who absorbs the insults and injuries of patriarchy to make for herself and her children something approaching a viable existence. The problem with this view is that it immediately raises the question of whether praise for Dolly merely endorses the equally masculine values of the worthy, suffering woman who lives for her children and through all adversity maintains a household and a family life. This view of women – the angel in the house – is as much part and parcel of conventional morality then as now. No real home, in bourgeois society (be it nineteenth-century Russia or twentieth-century Britain), should be without a Dolly: the wife who turns a blind eye to her husband's infidelities and plods along a worthy path of child care and domestic seclusion. Contemporary parallels to Dolly are numerous, famous and humble, and will no doubt remain until the day arrives on which women and men are required to accept alternative ways of ordering sexual relations.

Yet praise for Dolly is not, perhaps, as conservative as it may appear. It is undoubtedly good, in any moral community, to care for children and to give them the kind of attention and concerned interest that Dolly gives to her brood. Levin may mock Dolly's occasionally silly and pretentious attempts at educating her children (the lessons in French conversation that, for example, so irritate Levin and are, of course, particularly ironic in that it is Oblonsky's affair with the French governess that first brings into crisis the marriage of Dolly and Oblonsky) but her motives are those of real interest in the welfare of her children. So we cannot fault Dolly as a mother. What is more problematic is what is done – in terms of the moral evaluation of character – with that concern. Bourgeois society is, and was, enthusiastic about maternal devotion. Recently, feminist critics and theorists have made this concern the basis of an argument that maintains that women are innately better and morally more active than men. Women, it is argued, because of their concern for children, do not wage war, engage in military and aggressive acts, or seek the physical destruction or mutilation of others. That this is empirically the case is undeniable: women's domestic concerns, responsibilities, and seclusion have kept them away from all these activities. But the problem with this argument is whether or not it is the social circumstances of women's lives which give them the appearance of pacifism or some innate, given capacity – yet another instance of that nature or nurture argument which dogs all aspects of discussions of the differences between the roles and attitudes of men and women.

However the argument is resolved in the theoretical disputes within feminism, we have in Dolly a character who represents much that is admirable about human beings, be they male or female. But her demonstrated concern for others is not the sole reason for seeing her in such a favourable light: it is that Dolly's behaviour points the way towards social relationships, both between people of the same, and opposite, sexes, that is genuinely humanitarian and motivated by a belief in the essential goodness of all human beings. The act that above all others in *Anna Karenina* suggests that Dolly, of all the characters, has this capacity and a truly generous understanding of human behaviour, is her visit to Anna and Vronsky when the pair are living in social seclusion, almost isolation, on Vronsky's country estate. Dolly, it must be remembered, is a respectable married woman, of an unblemished reputation, with absolutely nothing to gain by a visit to a woman who has become a social outcast. The idea of pollution through social contact with those individuals who break social rules was ingrained in nineteenth-century bourgeois thinking. For example, at more or less the same time that Dolly was setting off to visit Anna, Elizabeth Gaskell was refusing to meet George Eliot, because Eliot was at the time living in an 'irregular' union with a married man. Elizabeth Gaskell was no doubt convinced that to visit George Eliot (in what was an immaculately respectable and well ordered household) would be so socially polluting that neither she, nor her Unitarian minister husband, would ever recover from the experience. More generously – to Elizabeth Gaskell that is – she was also perhaps concerned about appearing to sanction an arrangement which she felt was genuinely problematic and not in the best interests of the parties concerned. Whatever the reason, Elizabeth Gaskell – like Anna's previous acquaintances and friends – believed they would be ill-advised to continue their friendship with an erstwhile friend. Bourgeois society – like the Royal Enclosure at Ascot – is not an open society and must not be contaminated by the presence of those who are publicly known to have been involved in irregular sexual relations.

The significant phrase in the previous sentence is 'publicly known'. Bourgeois society neither cared, nor cares, about those individuals whose behaviour, however irregular and appalling, takes place in private. The second crucial qualification is that whilst bourgeois society cannot entertain publicly irregular sexuality, it makes different rules for men and women. Oblonsky can sleep with the French governess – or any other female – but women are judged more harshly and the price that is demanded of their irregular sexual unions is discretion, silence, and emotional distance. Vronsky's mother and other married aristocratic ladies may take lovers, but they are not supposed to enter into binding emotional or domestic relationships with them. The role that bourgeois women are supposed to play is to compensate for the inadequacies, shortcomings, and failings of bourgeois marriage in the same affectionless, and strictly regulated, terms as bourgeois men.

If Dolly had chosen to act by the code of her class and her gender she would not have set off to visit Anna. It was a visit in which Levin colluded – to the extent of lending Dolly his horses and his carriage – but it was not a visit that Levin himself (despite his admiration for Anna) chose to make, and he had profound doubts about whether Dolly should make the visit. In the event, his misgivings proved weaker than his sense of responsibility as a host. As a host, he was honour bound to secure comfortable and adequate travel for his guest. As Tolstoy describes the beginning of the visit:

> Dolly carried out her intention and went to see Anna. She was sorry to chagrin her sister and displease Levin. She quite understood how right the Levins were in not wishing to have anything to do with Vronsky; but she felt she must go and see Anna, and show her that the altered circumstances could not change her feelings towards her.
> To be independent of the Levins, Dolly sent to the village to hire horses for this expedition; but Levin heard of it and came to her in protest.
> 'What makes you suppose I disapprove of your going? And if I did I should find it still less pleasant if you would not use my horses,' he said. 'You never told me definitely that you were going. In the first place, it is not very nice for me to have you hiring horses in the village, and, what's of more importance, they'll undertake the job and never get you there. And if you don't wish to hurt my feelings you will make use of them.'[2]

Levin's view of the importance of the rules of hospitality therefore ensures a reasonably convenient, if inelegent (for Levin's horses and carriage are utilitarian rather than smart), journey for Dolly.

It is a journey that takes Dolly, metaphorically, to the site of sin. She, and she alone, is prepared to put aside bourgeois conventions and maintain a personal relationship which had mattered to her. What is all the more striking about the visit is that it demonstrates Dolly's absolute moral independence and honesty: Anna, it must be remembered, is the woman who at the beginning of the novel told Dolly a collection of half-truths and misleading fantasies about her husband's behaviour. Dolly has no particular reason to be grateful to Anna. Anna, when an admired and well placed society lady, did nothing to minimize Dolly's domestic difficulties and succeeded only in upsetting and wounding Kitty. But far from remembering the inadequacies of Anna's behaviour, and using Anna's fall from grace as an opportunity to extoll her own virtues and parade her own judgements, Dolly reaches out to a woman whose need for friendship, for emotional support, and for sisterly companionship is very real. The only comparable visit in the novel – that is, of individuals going out of their way to meet people of different and difficult circumstances – is that of Kitty and Levin to Levin's dying brother. Levin is originally hostile to this visit since he does not regard it as appropriate for his wife to visit his brother, and so run the risk of polluting contact with his brother's mistress. Kitty, however, is adamant. Yet what distinguishes Kitty's act from that of Dolly is that Kitty justifies her determination to accompany Levin in terms of her commitment to their marriage. She appeals to Levin: 'I feel it's my duty to be with my husband when he is in trouble.'

But Levin is not 'in trouble'. His brother is dying, and his brother has for years lived in an irregular union. Kitty's interpretation of the incident is therefore essentially a conventional one – Levin has somehow or other found himself with a problem, but the unity of husband and wife must be maintained, rather than conventional morality challenged. Determined to accompany her husband for conventional reasons, husband and wife set off – the husband still entertaining grave doubts about the presence of his wife:

> [Levin] . . . went dissatisfied at the bottom of his heart with her and with himself. He was dissatisfied with her because she could not bring herself to let him go when it was necessary (and how

strange to think that he, who such a short time ago had hardly dared to believe in the happiness of her loving him, now was unhappy because she loved him too much!); and was dissatisfied with himself for not having stood his ground. Still less could he with the least conviction agree that it did not matter if she came in contact with the woman who lived with his brother, and he was appalled to think of all the encounters that might take place. The mere idea of his wife, his Kitty, in the same room with a common wench set him shuddering with repulsion and horror.[3]

As it turns out, the visit is a success – insofar as a visit to a dying relative can be a success. Kitty busies herself by generally alleviating some of the physical discomfort of the dying man and Levin and his brother are able to spend the last hours of the latter's life together in peace and reconciliation. Even the dreaded 'common wench' behaves with propriety, keeps a proper distance from the gentry, and does not press personal and emotional claims that might have embarrassed anyone.

This visit confirms existing patterns of social life and expectations. Husband and wife face, as Christian marriage requires that they should, sickness and death together. 'For better, for worse' may not have been part of the ceremony of Russian Orthodox marriage in the nineteenth century but both Kitty and Levin are sufficiently aware of the proper duties of married Christians to know that married people are expected to stand by each other in times of difficulty and trouble. Throughout their marriage Kitty and Levin conjure with the inevitable contradictions and difficulties of an expectation about unity and obedience in marriage which is posed when the partners fundamentally disagree about what is wrong and right. Part of the fantasy world of *Anna Karenina* is Tolstoy's permission to Levin to be 'right' on a substantial number of occasions: since Levin is 'right', and his wife young and inexperienced, the unity of the marriage can be maintained as Levin occupies the potentially blissful position of being able to educate morally his young wife. So this marriage works, since a young wife is guided by an older man towards a more apparently reasonable, rational, and less frivolous interpretation of what constitutes right and wrong. If Anna is the fantasy sexual woman, the *femme fatale* of the male bourgeois imagination, then Kitty must also be the perfect female pupil for the missionary instincts and inclinations of educated bourgeois men. And it has to be said that in many ways Levin does epitomize the most tedious and pompous inclinations and attitudes of the nineteenth-century 'improving' husband, of whom the best example is Queen Victoria's husband Prince Albert. This marriage is documented by an extensive literature and correspondence. Prince Albert was determined to reform his wife. Although more or less the same age as Victoria and not apparently blessed with any real genius other than a capacity for obsessively hard work, the Prince decided early in his marriage that his wife had a head full of frivolous, if not dangerously silly ideas. He therefore embarked on a career of producing endless domestic memoranda, showering his bride with weekly reports on her behaviour and performance. Fired by a zeal for order and apparent coherence the Prince attempted to eradicate from his wife's conduct any trace of those habits in which he detected 'irrationality' or spontaneous reaction. Inevitably all he succeeded in doing was making the Queen more 'irrational' – the heavy hand of imposed order rapidly drove her repressed emotional energies into florid and exaggerated patterns.

The parallel of Queen Victoria and Prince Albert with Levin and Kitty is mentioned partly because of the endless fascination of the British Royal Family but substantially, and particularly in this context, because the Queen and Albert were real people – and lived out, and represented in reality precisely those tendencies that Levin and Kitty suggest in fiction. Levin, like Albert, was an improver. Like Albert, Levin believed in rational thinking, in the rational ordering of the world and in the enhancement of nature and the natural world by science. In both cases the motives of both individuals were perfectly sound, and generous. Albert did want to improve the condition of the majority of the British people, and Levin did want to better the lives of the peasants who depended upon him. But in both cases these excellent motives were accompanied by an attitude to emotional and sexual life that was, at best, inhibiting. Albert and Levin both longed for more 'reasonable' wives. Both

What is a Good Woman?

Victoria and Kitty resisted, but had to resist in ways that were ultimately degrading to both their husbands and themselves. So Kitty has to resort to tears to secure her point of view, and Queen Victoria's diaries and correspondence attest to the deep depressions and fluctuating moods which resulted from a relationship that could not allow or integrate emotional needs.

Anna herself is the most pathetic victim of these nineteenth-century marriages in which feeling is identified with women and rationality with men. Condemned to a life in which emotions and sexual expression are confined to the bourgeois bedroom – and a bedroom whose door only Karenin is allowed to open – Anna experiences mood swings and a desperate, and tragic, need for emotional companionship and expression. To the nineteenth-century male, Anna would have been – as she was to Tolstoy – a 'hysterical' woman, a woman driven mad by her sexuality and her emotional needs. Indeed, we might imagine Anna, in the real world, as one of those unhappy victims of nineteenth-century medicine who would have been subjected to a diagnosis of morbid hysteria and treated as if she were ill. In fiction her fate is rather worse, but what can be discerned is a parallel between Tolstoy's attitude towards Anna and that, say, of William Acton, or any of those nineteenth-century male doctors who were so ready to identify as hysterical any female behaviour – particularly the open and disturbing expression of an emotional state – which threatened to disturb the bourgeois social order. As a reaction to the potentially destructive power of emotional and sexual need, Anna has to be destroyed, and so becomes, not one of the feminist heroines of fiction, but one of its major, and most symbolic, victims.

Victims in fiction, like the real life victims of nineteenth (and twentieth) century medicine and psychiatry can engage our pity and sympathy and provoke rage against the ideologies and institutions which sustain these punitive practices. But while victims have this function, other people – both real and in fiction – should give us some idea of alternative behaviour. Of the women in *Anna Karenina*, it is Dolly who more than any other performs this role. Kitty is too locked into the ideology of bourgeois marriage to develop a critical view of the social world; moreover, Levin's own unswerving adherence to the code of proper bourgeois behaviour makes it unlikely that Kitty will develop a critical or reflective view of the institution within which she lives as the worshipped, powerless wife of a benign patriarch. Dolly, on the other hand, is married to a man who so obviously and comprehensively fails to meet the expectations of bourgeois society that she is forced to develop a more pragmatic appraisal of the possibilities of bourgeois marriage than her sister. Dolly, unlike Kitty, begins to ask questions about what she is doing, and why. For example, dearly as she loves her children, Dolly has to recognize that she has more children than she would wish, that she is unable to provide for them in a conventionally appropriate way, and that she, with little support from Oblonsky, is entirely responsible for the welfare and the care of her children. And yet despite severe difficulties and the physical and emotional suffering that Dolly endures (not the least of which is the death in infancy of two of her children) she remains sufficiently resilient and generous both towards her family and in her affections for Anna. Acts such as these suggest a moral capacity to recognize personal responsibility and to maintain concern for others even at risk to oneself.

Again, the contrast between Dolly's concern for her children, and her behaviour towards Anna, is underlined by Tolstoy in the references he makes to the conduct of others in these contexts. Anna's attitude to Ani – whatever the reason – is careless and neglectful. As suggested earlier, it is possible that Anna so deeply fears the repetition of the loss of a child that she is reluctant to develop a relationship with her daughter. Another interpretation, more closely compatible with the reading of Anna as singularly narcissistic, is that she sees in her daughter a competitor for male attention and praise. Furthermore, in patriarchal society, sons confirm the position and standing of their mothers since they give to their mothers a symbolic share in patriarchal power. Daughters, on the other hand, may well outshine their mothers in terms of their ability to attract men: narcissism is not flattered, but challenged, by this relationship. The helpless Ani, almost forgotten in her nursery, and at the mercy of the servants whom Dolly regards with the deepest mistrust, is typical of all those daughters feared by their mothers because of their close, and essential, access to male approval. Dolly exhibits no such attitude to her daughters; on the contrary, she is prepared to compromise her own appearance (certainly to give it a secondary status) in order to provide adequate clothing and education for her daughters. Furthermore, she actively cares for all her children, in that she is informed about them and recognizant of their tastes and differences. Anna adores Seriozha, it is true, but the reality of Seriozha is always something that surprises Anna. We might, therefore, assume that what Anna adores about her son is his youthful masculinity and enchanting appearance. The real child, less than the idealized vision of Anna's dream, but much more than the empty shadow of her fantasy, is as strange to Anna as Ani is to be.

If Anna represents the distorted, or conditioned, attitudes of women to their children in a world ruled by the interests and authority of husbands, then Oblonsky personifies the absent bourgeois father just as much as Anna is the absent bourgeois mother. Suffering from one of his fits of uncomfortable, if vague, guilt about his children and his family, Oblonsky reflects that:

> The children? In Petersburg children did not prevent their fathers from enjoying life. They were sent to school, and there was none of that silly nonsense such as was becoming prevalent in Moscow – Lvov's was a case in point – that the children should have all the luxuries of life and the parents nothing but work and anxiety. Here it was understood that a man should live for himself, as every civilized being should.[4]

The home- and child-centred family that Levin and Kitty represent, and that was to become the ideological model of the family in twentieth-century western Europe and North America, is a prospect that Oblonsky obviously finds deeply disturbing. As he rightly perceives, this arrangement would involve men in family obligations, responsibilities, and participation. If all these expectations were fulfilled – even within the general context of persistent inequalities between men and women – it would not attract men like Oblonsky whose understanding of family life was limited to physical comforts and a place to sleep.

Faced with the virtually constant absence of Oblonsky, Dolly maintains the household and family life. In doing so she does what millions of other women have done, and still do, in circumstances that are better, and worse, than those of Dolly. Like these silent women, Dolly creates a separate sphere for herself and her children. But it is still a separate sphere which has the generosity to care for others. Whilst Vronsky's family turn their back on Anna, and Anna's friends desert her, Dolly makes what is arguably one of the most sisterly, and most human, acts in fiction. Compare, for example, Dolly's unpatronizing attitude to Anna with that of Vronsky's cousin Betsy, and Vronsky's mother:

> Vronsky noticed that Betsy's enthusiasm waned when she learned that no divorce had as yet taken place.
>
> 'People will throw stories at me, I know,' she said, 'but I shall come and see Anna. I really must. You won't be here long, I suppose?'
>
> She did, in fact, call on Anna that very day; but her manner was very different from what it used to be. She was evidently proud of her courage, and wanted Anna to appreciate the fidelity of her friendship. She did not stay more than ten minutes, chattering society gossip, and on leaving she said:
>
> 'You have not told me when the divorce is to be. Of course I have ignored the conventions but other people will give you the cold shoulder until you are married. And that's so simple nowadays *la se fait*. So you are going on Friday. A pity we shan't see each other again.'
>
> From Betsy's tone Vronsky might have gathered what he had to expect from society; but he made another attempt in his own family. Of his mother he had no hopes. He knew that his mother, who had been so enthusiastic over Anna at his first meeting, would have no mercy on her now for having ruined her son's career. But he placed great hopes on Vanya, his brother's wife. He fancied that she would cast no stones, but in that simple and determined way of hers would come and see Anna, and receive her in her own house.[5]

Those hopes are to be rapidly disappointed in Vanya's firm, but uncompromising, rejection of Anna. Vanya says of Anna:

> 'You want me to go and see her, to ask her here, and to rehabilitate her in society; but do understand – I *cannot* do so. I have daughters growing up, and I must mix in society for my husband's sake.'[6]

Vanya, and Vronsky's mother, both illustrate two of the most commonplace, and depressing, facets of gender relations in bourgeois society: that the perceived need to maintain social order and social hierarchy will take precedent over human need, and that, in a choice between the needs of women and the needs of men, the needs of men will be given priority. Vanya knows quite well that Vronsky, and indeed Anna herself, would be deeply comforted by recognition and welcome. Yet, as she says, she has to act as her husband's wife, and maintain her daughters' marriageability. Receiving Anna would provoke suspicions about the moral tone of her household and her attitude to the world, both of which would have repercussions, social and material, in terms of her husband's career and the status of her daughters. Extending a hand of friendship to Anna would therefore entail a cost, social and financial, which Vanya is not prepared to risk. Faced with this rejection, Anna and Vronsky are plunged further into isolation which exacerbates their irritation with each other.

Women like Vanya act according to the dictates of patriarchal society. They disabuse us of the idea that there is some kind of 'natural' sisterhood between women, for they demonstrate a transparent determination to maintain the social structures and moral judgements of the patriarchal, bourgeois world. Women, just as much as men, will condemn other women – in fact it is often in the direct interests of women to maintain the distinction between 'good' and 'bad' women. Since patriarchal marriage rewards 'good' women, wives, and mothers, those same women have to make publicly certain that deviants are known as such. The fragile, yet infinitely subtle weapon of female respectability has to be kept carefully intact, lest some rashly liberal interpretation of the ambiguity of many human actions should blur the distinction between good and bad. So women – Vanya, and to a certain extent Kitty – are forced into moralistic positions consistent with a code that inevitably reinforces the subordination of women. Dolly, alone of all the women in the novel, neither judges nor condemns. She sighs over Oblonsky's infidelities, yet quite accurately recognizes that his other failings – in particular his financial irresponsibility – are equally relevant, and potentially damaging to her situation. She does not snap at Kitty (although Kitty unkindly reminds her of Oblonsky's wanderings) and so does not remind Kitty that whatever her charms, they were not enough to sustain Vronsky's interest once he had set eyes on Anna. All in all, Dolly acts well. She acts as a morally autonomous person who is not afraid to risk adverse judgements and hence is not subservient to an empty morality. Far from being conditioned, like Anna, by patriarchal ideology in its most repressive and distorting forms, Dolly has developed a judgement that can suggest to readers of *Anna Karenina* a model for reflection and thought.

Escaping the doll's house in which society imprisons women is a matter of multiple strategies, not the least of which is the destruction of the doll's house itself. Financial independence, civil rights, and control over fertility are all strategies which provide partial routes out of the childish dependence to which women like Kitty are confined. But a significant strategy, and a significant part of the world which has to be re-constructed and re-thought outside the limited, and limiting structures of the patriarchal family, is defining a morality independent of material and domestic constraints – a morality that provides comparison and support and does not distinguish between women and men. Despite her situation, Dolly goes some way towards meeting the expectations of this moral ideal. The dowdy wife, cast aside and ignored by her husband, is paradoxically relatively free to act as a mature and independent human being. Free from male approval and control, and free from the equally imprisoning need for male sexual interest, Dolly becomes a human being who cannot fail to impress readers by her bravery and resilience. Generous and concerned, responsible and consistent, she suggests the moral and human possibilities that exist alongside the conventional emotional and domestic arrangements of bourgeois society.

NOTES

CHAPTER ONE

1. Leavis, F. R. (1967) 'Anna Karenina: thought and significance in a great creative work', in F. R. Leavis *Anna Karenina and Other Essays*, New York: Simon & Schuster, pp. 20–1.

2. Bayley, John (1986) ' "This novel ... " *Anna Karenina*', in John Bayley *Tolstoy and the Novel*, London: Chatto & Windus, p. 205.

3. Tolstoy, Leo (1964) *Anna Karenina*, Harmondsworth: Penguin, p. 75.

4. ibid., p. 70.

5. ibid., p. 70.

6. ibid., p. 668.

7. ibid., p. 669.

8. Engels, Friedrich (1964) *The Origin of the Family, Private Property and the State*, Moscow: Foreign Languages Publishing House, pp. 109–10.

9. Tolstoy, Leo *Anna Karenina*, p. 853.

10. ibid., p. 119.

11. ibid., p. 127.

12. ibid., pp. 106–7.

13. Freud, Sigmund (1986) 'On the universal tendency to debasement in the sphere of love', in Sigmund Freud *On Sexuality: Three Essays on the Theory of Sexuality and Other Works*, Harmondsworth: Penguin, p. 258.

14. Wilson, Elizabeth (1986) 'Forbidden Love', in Elizabeth Wilson *Hidden Agendas*, London: Tavistock, p. 179.

CHAPTER TWO

1. Tolstoy, Leo (1964) *Anna Karenina*, Harmondsworth: Penguin, p. 15.
2. ibid., p. 82.
3. ibid., pp. 84–5.
4. ibid., p. 772.
5. ibid., p. 327.
6. ibid., p. 328.
7. ibid., p. 204.
8. ibid., p. 311.
9. ibid., p. 760.
10. ibid., p. 784.

CHAPTER THREE

1. Polner, Tikhon (1946) *Tolstoy and his Wife*, London: Cape, p.187.
2. ibid., p. 210.
3. Tolstoy, Leo (1964) *Anna Karenina*, Harmonsworth: Penguin, pp. 481–2.
4. ibid., p. 736.
5. ibid., p. 141.
6. ibid., p. 599.
7. ibid., p. 515.
8. ibid., p. 516.
9. ibid., p. 525.
10. ibid., p. 140.
11. ibid., p. 647.

CHAPTER FOUR

1. Ruddick, Sara (1982) 'Maternal Thinking', in Barrie Thorne and Marilyn Yalom (eds) *Rethinking the Family*, London: Longman, pp. 84–5.
2. Tolstoy, Leo (1964) *Anna Karenina*, Harmondsworth: Penguin, p. 636.
3. ibid., p. 516.
4. ibid., p. 761.
5. ibid., p. 557.
6. ibid., p. 558.